加拿大稅務
輕鬆學

2023版

 廖建勛 會計師 著
Richar RichLife

Chapter 3 第三章 加拿大個人稅務

Chapter 4　第四章 加拿大公司稅務

自序

加拿大（Canada）全球領土第二大，僅次於俄羅斯，是一個位於北美洲北部的國家，屬於西半球及北半球，其領土西臨太平洋，東瀕大西洋，北接北冰洋，有部分領土位於北極圈內。該國首都為渥太華，主要城市有溫哥華、多倫多與蒙特婁等。

加拿大是世界上擁有最多元化種族及文化的國家之一，也是一個移民國家，約四分之一的公民出生於境外。

加拿大更常被《富比士》評比為最宜居的國家名單之中。

也正因加拿大如此受到世界各地的喜愛及嚮往，所以前往加拿大留學、工作及移民都是相當熱門的。因此，無論是欲前往加拿大留學、工作甚至是移民的朋友，常會遇到加拿大稅務的問題。而市面上介紹加拿大的中文書籍並不多，為了解決在加拿大當地的稅務問題，所以本人提筆寫起這本拙作，希望本書的內容能滿足讀者的需求，不再因為報稅季來臨而難以入眠。最後，要由衷感謝家人同仁對本人的支持及幫助。

第一章
加拿大
稅制概述

　　加拿大（Canada）是全球面積第二大國家，有部分領土位於北極圈內。該國首都為渥太華，主要城市有溫哥華、多倫多與蒙特婁等。加拿大是世界上擁有最多元化種族及文化的國家之一，擁有600 多種不同的文化以及不同背景的人，加拿大政府更通過官方政策維護和加強多元文化，是世界上移民率最高的國家之一，約四分之一的公民出生於境外。加拿大被《富比士》列於2020年退休宜居國的名單中。大約有 18% 的加拿大人能精通英法雙語，魁北克省是加拿大唯一以法語為主的省份，聯邦政府提供的所有服務都提供兩種語言，幾乎所有產品都有英文和法文標籤和包裝。

　　加拿大以高福利政策自豪，然而高福利往往伴隨著高稅收，加拿大屬聯邦、地方稅收分權型國家，類似於美國，分為聯邦、省和地方三級徵稅制度，聯邦和省各有相對獨立的稅收立法權，地方的稅收立法權由省賦予。本章節將簡介加拿大的各項稅制及節稅相關福利政策，本書中所提金額，未特別註明皆以加幣為單位，表格內之各項金額雖已儘可能更新，惟仍可能隨加拿大日後政策而調整，請讀者務必留意。

從徵稅種類劃分來看，聯邦政府徵收的稅種主要有：

■聯邦所得稅　　　　■聯邦貨物服務稅

■消費稅　　　　　　■關稅

■聯邦資本稅

省政府徵收的稅種主要有：

■省所得稅　　　　　■省銷售稅

■省資本稅　　　　　■不動產轉讓稅

■資源稅

 # 第一節　個人稅

壹、稅務居民：

　　加拿大的納稅義務人認定原則是什麼呢?您是否需要繳納所得稅，不只是取決於是否是加拿大永久居民或是公民，一般而言，只要你在一年中於加拿大逗留超過183日，就自動定義為稅務居民，須於每年的報稅季節-三月至四月報稅。加拿大的稅務居民必須申報在全世界獲得的收入。相反，非稅務居民只須申報在加拿大的收入和來自加拿大財產的收益，非稅務居民採屬地主義 (Territoriality Principle)。

　　若是第一次入境加拿大的新移民，報到後隨即返國，並沒有實際在加拿大長久居住，則不屬於稅務居民，無須報稅及申報海外資產；若是第一次入境加拿大就長久居住的新移民，並且每年居住累計超過183天，就會被認定為稅務居民，需要報稅及申報海外資產。

貳、收入及費用：

一、全球課稅

　　不論在任何地方，只要是加拿大居民都符合全球課稅原則，加拿大居民必須根據其在世界各國所獲得的收入繳納所得稅，收入認定採屬人主義(Nationality Principle)，個人應繳納的是個人所得稅，就像是台灣每年5月須申報的綜所稅，加拿大執行的是「自動申報」報稅制度，納稅人有責任向稅務局申報所有收入，並自行計算稅金。

加拿大個人所得稅應課稅收入主要有以下五種:
■**Employment Income 薪資所得：**

在加拿大境內或海外透過工作獲取的薪資收入，包括獎金、加給津貼。

■Investment Income 投資所得：

透過財產而獲取的收入，包括利息、股利、房產租金。

■Business Income 生意所得：

不論是獨資或合夥，透過經商做生意的營運收入。

■Capital Gains 資本所得：

企業營運收入以外與企業資本相關收入，例如出售固定資產所獲取的收入。

■FAPI(Foreign Accrual Property Income) 海外受控公司被動投資所得：

獨資或合夥擁有海外受控公司50%以上控制權，皆須在稅單內填報其在海外受控公司所佔比例的投資收入。

二、稅前扣除額

所有收入加總後會得到所得總額，跟台灣一樣計算所得稅時，會有一些扣除額可以減免。

加拿大所得稅可扣除額為以下四項：

■Child Care Expenses 育兒扣除額：

撫養17歲以下兒童可減稅,像是台灣報稅也可以申報撫養人數減免稅金。

■Deductible Interest 可減除利息:

非購置私人資產所產生的利息可扣除,例如:貸款做生意。

■RRSP(Registered Retirement Savings Plan)
註冊退休儲蓄計劃:

存入退休儲蓄帳戶的收入可暫免報稅,儲蓄帳戶裡的金額隨時可提領,或是到了71歲年底前,RRSP會強制期滿,必須選擇一次提領認列收入或是分期提領延遲認列收入再次達到節稅效果。

■其他扣除額:

比如商業投資損失、搬遷費、居家辦公費用等。

三、個人免稅額

在計算加拿大所得稅稅金的時候,可以有多達數十種的個人可扣除項目。

主要分為以下五項:
■Personal Exemptions 個人扣除額:

可從所得淨額中扣減,包括基本扣除額、已婚扣除額、高齡扣除額、殘疾扣除額、就業扣除額、學費扣除額等等。

■**Spousal Exemptions 已婚扣除額：**

已婚人士收入合併一起申報所得稅，若是配偶收入在$13,808
以下可扣除。

■**Age Exemptions 65歲高齡扣除額：**

淨收入超過$38,900扣除額遞減，超過$90,000無扣除額。

■**Disability Amount 身心障礙扣除額：**

納稅人或受撫養親屬屬身心障礙人士可扣除額。

■**Tuition Fees 學費扣除額：**

受撫養子女就學學費可扣除額，海外就學也可扣除。

但是要如何知道自己要繳多少稅呢？你必須知道自己的「所得
淨額」，扣除個人免稅額後就是你的「課稅所得」。先來看看計
算公式：

$$所得淨額＝所得總額-可扣除額$$
$$課稅所得＝所得淨額-個人免稅額$$

四、常見申報表格：

在加拿大不論是新移民或是工作者，在每年的報稅季時，因為
報稅細節繁瑣，大多會選擇委託專業會計師申報，若是有委託會
計師代為申報的話，都會收到會計師請你提供T4表格及其他相關
資料，好協助你做完整申報，報稅時常見表格介紹及用途如下：

■T1134：海外企業申報

Canada Revenue Agency / **Agence du revenu du Canada**

Information Return Relating to Controlled and Non-Controlled Foreign Affiliates
(2021 and later taxation years)
T1134 Summary Form

- Use this version of the return for taxation years that begin after 2020.
- For T1134 returns that are filed in respect of taxation years that begin before 2021, please use the previous version of the T1134 form as released on November 28, 2017.
- For any amended T1134 return, please use the same version as the original T1134 return filed.
- Refer to the instructions before you complete the T1134 Summary and Supplements.
- A separate supplement must be filed for each foreign affiliate. However, do not file a supplement for a "dormant" or "inactive" foreign affiliate.
- Refer to the instructions for the definition of dormant or inactive foreign affiliates.
- References on this return to the foreign affiliate or the affiliate refer to the foreign affiliate for which the reporting entity is filing a supplement.
- If you are reporting on a partnership, references to year or taxation year should be read as fiscal period.
- If you need more space to report information, you can use attachments.
- If an election has been made to use functional currency, state the alphabetic currency code of the functional currency. (Note: only certain corporations can elect to report in a functional currency - see instructions.) . . . .

Do not use this area

If this is an amended return, tick this box. ☐

Is this T1134 Summary filed for one reporting entity or a group of reporting entities that are related to each other? (see instructions)

☐ One reporting entity   ☐ A group of reporting entities that are related to each other

If this T1134 Summary is filed for a group of reporting entities that are related to each other, indicate which entity is the representative reporting entity for the related group in Section 1 – reporting entity information.

Part I – Identification
Section 1 – Reporting entity information

Tick a box to indicate who you are reporting for, and complete the areas that apply (please print)

	First name	Last name	Initial(s)	Social insurance number (SIN)
☐ Individual				

	Corporation's name		Business number (BN)	
☐ Corporation				R C

	Trust's name		Trust's account number	
☐ Trust			T –	–

	Partnership's name		Partnership's account number	Partnership Code
☐ Partnership			R Z	

Reporting entity's address

_____
Number   Street

_____
City   Province/territory or state   Postal or ZIP code   Country code

Reporting entity's NAICS code(s) (6 digits)   1. _____   2. _____   3. _____   4. _____

For what taxation year are you filing this form?   From   Year Month Day   To   Year Month Day

Does this period include 2 or more short taxation years? (see instructions)   Yes ☐   No ☐

Number of supplements attached _____

Section 2 – Certification

Person to contact for more information (please print)

First name	Last name	Telephone number

I, _____ , certify that the information given on these T1134 Summary and Supplements are, to the best of my knowledge,
(Print name)
correct and complete.

Date	Authorized signing officer's, or representative's signature	Position, title, officer's rank

■T1135：海外資產申報

Canada Revenue Agency	Agence du revenu du Canada

Foreign Income Verification Statement

Protected B when completed
For departmental use.

- This form must be used for the 2015 and later taxation years.
- Complete and file this form if at any time in the year the total cost amount to the reporting taxpayer of all specified foreign property was more than $100,000 (Canadian).
- If an election has been made to use a functional currency (see attached instructions), state the elected functional currency code. . . . .
- See attached instructions for more information about completing this form.

If this is an amended return, tick this box.

Identification

Tick a box to indicate who you are reporting for, and complete the areas that apply.

Individual	First name	Last name	Initial
	Social insurance number	Individual code 1 2
Corporation	Corporation's name	Business number R C
Trust	Trust's name	Account number T -
Partnership	Partnership's name	Partnership code 1 2 3	Partnership's account number R Z

Reporting entity's address

No.   Street

City   Province or territory   Postal code   Country code

For what taxation year are you filing this form?   From Year Month Day to Year Month Day

Tick the appropriate box that applies for the taxation year:

☐ If the total cost of all specified foreign property held at any time during the year exceeds $100,000 but was less than $250,000, you are required to complete either Part A or Part B;

☐ If the total cost of all specified foreign property held at any time during the year was $250,000 or more, you are required to complete Part B.

Part A: Simplified reporting method

For each type of property that applies to you, tick the appropriate box.

Type of property:

Funds held outside Canada . . . . ☐
Shares of non-resident corporations (other than foreign affiliates) . . . . ☐
Indebtedness owed by non-resident . . . . ☐
Interests in non-resident trusts . . . . ☐
Real property outside Canada (other than personal use and real estate used in an active business) . . . . . ☐
Other property outside Canada . . . . ☐
Property held in an account with a Canadian registered securities dealer or a Canadian trust company . . . . ☐

Country code:

Select the top three countries based on the maximum cost amount of specified foreign property held during the year. Enter the country codes in the boxes below:

Gross income from all specified foreign property $ _____

Gain(loss) from the disposition from all specified foreign property $ _____

Privacy Act, personal information bank number CRA PPU 035

■T2202：學費扣除額

Canada Revenue Agency	Agence du revenu du Canada		**Protected B** when completed **Protégé B** une fois rempli

Tuition and Enrolment Certificate
Certificat pour frais de scolarité et d'inscription

For student / Pour étudiant **1**

Year
Année

Name and address of designated educational institution Nom et adresse de l'établissement d'enseignement	11 School type Catégorie d'école	12 Flying school or club École ou club de pilotage
	14 Student number Numéro d'étudiant	15 Filer Account Number Numéro de compte du déclarant

13 Name of program or course Nom du programme ou du cours	Session periods Périodes d'études	19 From YY/MM De AA/MM	20 To YY/MM À AA/MM	21 Number of months part-time Nombre de mois à temps partiel	22 Number of months full-time Nombre de mois à temps plein	23 Eligible tuition fees, part-time and full-time Frais de scolarité admissibles pour études à temps partiel et à temps plein
Student Name Nom de l'étudiant	1					
	2					
Student address Adresse de l'étudiant	3					
	4					
	Totals / Totaux 24			25	26	

Information for students: See the back of Certificate 1. If you want to transfer all or part of your tuition amount, complete the back of Certificate 2

Renseignements pour les étudiants : Lisez le verso du certificat 1. Si vous désirez transférer une partie ou la totalité de vos frais de scolarité, remplissez le verso du certificat 2.

17 Social insurance number (SIN) Numéro d'assurance sociale (NAS)

See the privacy notice on the next page.
Consultez l'avis de confidentialité à la page suivante.

T2202 (21)

Canada

Canada Revenue Agency	Agence du revenu du Canada		**Protected B** when completed **Protégé B** une fois rempli

Tuition and Enrolment Certificate
Certificat pour frais de scolarité et d'inscription

For student / Pour étudiant **2**

Year
Année

Name and address of designated educational institution Nom et adresse de l'établissement d'enseignement	11 School type Catégorie d'école	12 Flying school or club École ou club de pilotage
	14 Student number Numéro d'étudiant	15 Filer Account Number Numéro de compte du déclarant

13 Name of program or course Nom du programme ou du cours	Session periods Périodes d'études	19 From YY/MM De AA/MM	20 To YY/MM À AA/MM	21 Number of months part-time Nombre de mois à temps partiel	22 Number of months full-time Nombre de mois à temps plein	23 Eligible tuition fees, part-time and full-time Frais de scolarité admissibles pour études à temps partiel et à temps plein
Student Name Nom de l'étudiant	1					
	2					
Student address Adresse de l'étudiant	3					
	4					
	Totals / Totaux 24			25	26	

Information for students: See the back of Certificate 1. If you want to transfer all or part of your tuition amount, complete the back of Certificate 2

Renseignements pour les étudiants : Lisez le verso du certificat 1. Si vous désirez transférer une partie ou la totalité de vos frais de scolarité, remplissez le verso du certificat 2.

17 Social insurance number (SIN) Numéro d'assurance sociale (NAS)

See the privacy notice on the next page.
Consultez l'avis de confidentialité à la page suivante.

T2202 (21)

Canada

■TL11A：海外大學學費扣除額

		Tuition and Enrolment Certificate – University Outside Canada	Protected B when completed
Canada Revenue Agency	Agence du revenu du Canada		Year: 20____

This certificate is used to certify eligibility for claiming tuition fees of a student attending a university outside Canada. Administrators of educational institutions outside Canada can refer to **Information sheet RC190**, Information for Educational Institutions Outside Canada, at **canada.ca/forms-publications** for details on completing this certificate.

Part 1 – Educational institution's certification

	A Session periods				B Number of months for **part-time**	C Number of months for **full-time**
	From		To			
	Year	Month	Year	Month		
Name of educational institution						
Address of educational institution						
Name of program or course						
Student's name						
	Total ▶					

I certify that:
- the student was registered as a student at this educational institution in a university course as described above during the periods indicated
- out of the total fees paid for the year, $ _____ is the amount paid for tuition, mandatory ancillary fees that all students have to pay (such as fees for health services or athletics other than student association fees), admission, use of a library or a laboratory, examinations, and for getting a degree
- no part of the above amount was levied for other things such as transportation, parking, books, supplies, special equipment, meals, lodging, or initiation or entrance fees for professional organizations
- the total eligible tuition fees indicated above include the eligible tuition fees paid by scholarship income

_____   _____   _____
Authorized officer's name and title (print)   Authorized officer's signature   Date

Part 2 – Information for Students

- To calculate your available tuition, education, and textbook amount, fill out federal Schedule 11, Federal Tuition, Education, and Textbook Amounts and Canada Training Credit. Depending on where you live, you also may need to fill out a provincial or territorial Schedule (S11).
- If you want to transfer unused current year amounts to one designated individual, complete Part 3 of this certificate. If you did not reside in the same province or territory as the designated individual on December 31, special rules may apply.
- For more information, see **Guide P105**, Students and Income Tax, and **Information sheet RC192**, Information for Students – Educational Institutions Outside Canada, at **canada.ca/cra-forms-publications**.
- Do **not** send this certificate with your Income Tax and Benefit Return. Keep the certificate in case we ask to see it.

Part 3 – Student's authorization to transfer tuition, education, and textbook amounts

I designate _____ , my _____ , to claim:
                        Individual's name   Relationship to you

(1) $ _____ on line 32400 of their **Income Tax and Benefit Return**, or on line 36000 of their **federal Schedule 2**, as
        Federal tuition amount   applicable

(2) $ _____ on line 58600 of their **provincial** or **territorial Form 428**, or on line 59090 of their **provincial** or **territorial**
        Provincial or territorial   **Schedule (S2)**, as applicable
        amount

Note 1: Line (1) above cannot be more than the maximum transferable amount on your **federal Schedule 11**.
Note 2: Line (2) above cannot be more than the maximum transferable amount of your **provincial** or **territorial Schedule (S11)**. If you resided in Quebec, Alberta, Ontario or Saskatchewan on December 31, you are not required to fill out line (2) above.

_____   _____   _____
Student's signature   Social insurance number   Date

See the privacy notice on your return.

TL11A E (21)   (Ce formulaire est disponible en français.)   Canada

■T3：基金收入

■T4：薪資所得

■T4A：退休金、老人年金

■T5：利息、股息收入

| Canada Revenue Agency / Agence du revenu du Canada | T5 | Statement of Investment Income / État des revenus de placement | Year / Année | Protected B / Protégé B when completed / une fois rempli |

Dividends from Canadian corporations – Dividendes de sociétés canadiennes			Federal credit – Crédit fédéral		
24 Actual amount of eligible dividends / Montant réel des dividendes déterminés	25 Taxable amount of eligible dividends / Montant imposable des dividendes déterminés	26 Dividend tax credit for eligible dividends / Crédit d'impôt pour dividendes déterminés	13 Interest from Canadian sources / Intérêts de source canadienne	18 Capital gains dividends / Dividendes sur gains en capital	
10 Actual amount of dividends other than eligible dividends / Montant réel des dividendes autres que des dividendes déterminés	11 Taxable amount of dividends other than eligible dividends / Montant imposable des dividendes autres que des dividendes déterminés	12 Dividend tax credit for dividends other than eligible dividends / Crédit d'impôt pour dividendes autres que des dividendes déterminés	21 Report Code / Code du feuillet	22 Recipient identification number / Numéro d'identification du bénéficiaire	23 Recipient type / Type de bénéficiaire

Other information (see the back) / Autres renseignements (lisez le dos)

| Box / Case | Amount / Montant | Box / Case | Amount / Montant | Box / Case | Amount / Montant |

Recipient's name (last name first) and address – Nom, prénom et adresse du bénéficiaire

Payer's name and address – Nom et adresse du payeur

Currency and identification codes / Codes de devise et d'identification ▶ 27 Foreign currency / Devises étrangères 28 Transit – Succursale 29 Recipient account number / Numéro de compte du bénéficiaire

For information, see the back. Pour obtenir des renseignements, lisez le dos.

See the privacy notice on your return./ Consultez l'avis de confidentialité dans votre déclaration.
T5 (09/21)

| Canada Revenue Agency / Agence du revenu du Canada | T5 | Statement of Investment Income / État des revenus de placement | Year / Année | Protected B / Protégé B when completed / une fois rempli |

Dividends from Canadian corporations – Dividendes de sociétés canadiennes			Federal credit – Crédit fédéral		
24 Actual amount of eligible dividends / Montant réel des dividendes déterminés	25 Taxable amount of eligible dividends / Montant imposable des dividendes déterminés	26 Dividend tax credit for eligible dividends / Crédit d'impôt pour dividendes déterminés	13 Interest from Canadian sources / Intérêts de source canadienne	18 Capital gains dividends / Dividendes sur gains en capital	
10 Actual amount of dividends other than eligible dividends / Montant réel des dividendes autres que des dividendes déterminés	11 Taxable amount of dividends other than eligible dividends / Montant imposable des dividendes autres que des dividendes déterminés	12 Dividend tax credit for dividends other than eligible dividends / Crédit d'impôt pour dividendes autres que des dividendes déterminés	21 Report Code / Code du feuillet	22 Recipient identification number / Numéro d'identification du bénéficiaire	23 Recipient type / Type de bénéficiaire

Other information (see the back) / Autres renseignements (lisez le dos)

| Box / Case | Amount / Montant | Box / Case | Amount / Montant | Box / Case | Amount / Montant |

Recipient's name (last name first) and address – Nom, prénom et adresse du bénéficiaire

Payer's name and address – Nom et adresse du payeur

Currency and identification codes / Codes de devise et d'identification ▶ 27 Foreign currency / Devises étrangères 28 Transit – Succursale 29 Recipient account number / Numéro de compte du bénéficiaire

For information, see the back. Pour obtenir des renseignements, lisez le dos.

See the privacy notice on your return./ Consultez l'avis de confidentialité dans votre déclaration.
T5 (09/21)

| Canada Revenue Agency / Agence du revenu du Canada | T5 | Statement of Investment Income / État des revenus de placement | Year / Année | Protected B / Protégé B when completed / une fois rempli |

Dividends from Canadian corporations – Dividendes de sociétés canadiennes			Federal credit – Crédit fédéral		
24 Actual amount of eligible dividends / Montant réel des dividendes déterminés	25 Taxable amount of eligible dividends / Montant imposable des dividendes déterminés	26 Dividend tax credit for eligible dividends / Crédit d'impôt pour dividendes déterminés	13 Interest from Canadian sources / Intérêts de source canadienne	18 Capital gains dividends / Dividendes sur gains en capital	
10 Actual amount of dividends other than eligible dividends / Montant réel des dividendes autres que des dividendes déterminés	11 Taxable amount of dividends other than eligible dividends / Montant imposable des dividendes autres que des dividendes déterminés	12 Dividend tax credit for dividends other than eligible dividends / Crédit d'impôt pour dividendes autres que des dividendes déterminés	21 Report Code / Code du feuillet	22 Recipient identification number / Numéro d'identification du bénéficiaire	23 Recipient type / Type de bénéficiaire

Other information (see the back) / Autres renseignements (lisez le dos)

| Box / Case | Amount / Montant | Box / Case | Amount / Montant | Box / Case | Amount / Montant |

Recipient's name (last name first) and address – Nom, prénom et adresse du bénéficiaire

Payer's name and address – Nom et adresse du payeur

Currency and identification codes / Codes de devise et d'identification ▶ 27 Foreign currency / Devises étrangères 28 Transit – Succursale 29 Recipient account number / Numéro de compte du bénéficiaire

For information, see the back. Pour obtenir des renseignements, lisez le dos.

See the privacy notice on your return./ Consultez l'avis de confidentialité dans votre déclaration.
T5 (09/21)

■RC66：兒童補助金

<table>
<tr><td>■◆■ Canada Revenue Agency</td><td>Agence du revenu du Canada</td><td>Protected B when completed</td></tr>
</table>

Canada Child Benefits Application
includes federal, provincial, and territorial programs

Find out if this form is for you

Fill out this form to apply for the Canada child benefit and register your children for the goods and services tax/harmonized sales tax (GST/HST) credit, the climate action incentive payment (CAIP) and related federal, provincial, or territorial programs the Canada Revenue Agency (CRA) administers. You can also use this form if you started a shared-custody situation for one or more children.

Do not fill out this form if you already applied using My Account on the CRA website or when you registered the birth of your newborn with your province or territory (except Yukon and Nunavut).

Who should fill out this form

The person who is **primarily responsible** for the care and upbringing of the child should apply (see "Primarily responsible for the care and upbringing of the child" on page 3).

When a child resides with a female parent in the home, the female parent is usually considered to be primarily responsible for the child and should apply. However, if the child's other parent is primarily responsible, they should apply and attach a signed letter from the female parent stating that the other parent with whom she resides is primarily responsible for all the children in the home. If the child lives with same-sex parents, only one parent should apply for all the children in the home.

For more information

For more information on the Canada child benefit, including eligibility requirements, go to **canada.ca/cra-benefits**, see Booklet T4114, Canada Child Benefit, or call **1-800-387-1193**. From outside Canada or the United States, call **1-613-940-8495**. We accept collect calls by automated response.

Step 1 – Your information

Social insurance number (SIN):

If you do not have a SIN, see Booklet T4114, Canada Child Benefit, under "How to apply."

First name:

Last name:

Date of birth: Year   Month   Day

Your language of correspondence: ☐ English   ☐ Français

Phone numbers: Home: _____   Work: _____   Ext: _____   Cell: _____

Step 2 – Your address

Mailing address

Apt. No. – Street No., Street name, PO Box, RR:

City:

Province or territory (or country if outside Canada):

Postal or ZIP code:

Have you moved from a different province or territory within the last 12 months?   ☐ Yes   ☐ No

If **yes**, enter the previous province or territory and the date you moved: Date: ___ Year Month Day

Home address   ☐ Same as mailing address

Apt. No. – Street No., Street name, RR:

City:

Province or territory (or country if outside Canada):

Postal or ZIP code:

RC66 E (22)   (Ce formulaire est disponible en français.)   Page 1 of 6   Canada

第二節 福利政策

　　高稅收伴隨著加拿大擁有引以為傲的優越福利政策，一路從出生照顧到退休生活，包含由政府主導的育兒、教育、退休等福利制度，以及私人或雇主主導的醫療、退休金方案，除了員工可以獲得福利，雇主也可以達到節稅的目的，並訂定多項儲蓄計劃，不僅鼓勵國民及早儲蓄替未來做準備，更可同步獲得節稅的效益，以下是加拿大主要的福利政策：

壹、育兒教育：

■National Child Benefit 兒童福利金：

又稱牛奶金，低收家庭可以領取的養育津貼。

■Child Care Subsidy 托兒補助金：

在加拿大，6 歲前小孩的學前教育是自費的，而且費用很貴。導致很多低收入家庭無力把小孩送去接受早期教育，因此政府就專門撥款成立托兒補助金。

■Canada Learning Bond 加拿大教育基金：

針對2004年1月1日後出生並領有兒童補助的兒童，一次性發給

$500教育基金，每年另發給$100教育基金至15歲為止。

■RESP(Registered Education Savings Plan)

註冊教育儲蓄計劃：

父母或祖父母可以將教育儲蓄費存入教育儲蓄計劃的主管機構，雖然無法作為減稅用途，但是所產生的利息收入則不需課稅。

Tips

父母或祖父母可以將教育儲蓄費存入教育儲蓄計劃的主管機構，雖然無法作為減稅用途，但是所產生的利息收入則不需課稅。存款及利息累積起來用作未來子女或孫子女的教育費，包括學費、書籍費、住宿費、交通費等等。

每一受益人終身可領取的教育金額度上限為$50,000，每年存入多少金額不受限制，但是聯邦政府會依每年存入金額提供20%的額外助學金，最高$500(終身助學金最高$7,200)，因此為了獲取最多助學金，至少每年存入$2,500(2500*20%=500)，最少存入15年(500*15>7,200)。

1998年以前，若是受益人沒有持續進修課程，導致無法使用這筆教育儲蓄金，將會退還本金，但會損失這段期間的利息收入。1998年以後，允許將本金轉入受益人RRSP(退休儲蓄計劃)，最高上限$50,000；利息部分則需認列收入，並課徵20%特別稅，而助學金部分則全數退還政府。

■**In-trust Account 私人信託計劃：**

除了註冊教育儲蓄計劃可以分散收入以外，透過私人信託計劃也能達到分散收入給子女的目的，且不受額度、期限、提取限制。

貳、退休計劃：

■**RRSP(Registered Retirement Savings Plan)**
註冊退休儲蓄計劃：

加拿大政府為鼓勵居民替退休計劃做準備，及早儲蓄退休養老金，存入退休儲蓄帳戶的收入可暫免報稅，待提領出來時再行申報收入。

Tips

加拿大政府為鼓勵居民替退休計劃做準備，及早儲蓄退休養老金，存入退休儲蓄帳戶的收入可暫免報稅，待提領出來時再行申報收入。尚未退休時因為還有收入，所以所得稅率較高，待退休後提領出來時，可能已經沒有其他收入，因此稅率會比年輕時低，就可以達成節稅的目的。

每年的存款是有額度限制的，會以去年勞工收入的18%計算最高限額，當年度限額沒用完的話可以加在未來存款限額使用，儲蓄帳戶裡的金額隨時可提領，或是到了71歲年底前，RRSP會強制期滿，必須選擇一次提領認列收入或是分期提領延遲認列收入再次達到節稅效果。

■**Reverse Mortgage 房屋抵押貸款：**

退休後可以透過房屋抵押貸款獲取日常生活費用的一種方式，
待房屋出售時再一次性償還本金及利息。

■**OAS(Old Age Security) 老人年金：**

加拿大政府發給老年人口的退休補助津貼，若是定居加拿大未
滿40年，則可領取的津貼依比例遞減。

> Tips
>
> 加拿大政府發給老年人口的退休補助津貼，若是定居加拿大未滿40
> 年，則可領取的津貼依比例遞減，凡符合以下條件，接可申請領取此
> 筆老人養老津貼。
>
> 一、年滿65歲以上加拿大居民(2023年4月開始，須年滿67歲以上)
>
> 二、(一) 申請時居住在加拿大且住滿10年(18歲以後開始計算)
>
> （二)申請時居住於加拿大境外且境內住滿20年(18歲以後開始
> 計算)

■**Allowance 高齡配偶津貼：**

若是配偶已在領取OAS及GIS補助，則可以請領此筆高齡配偶
津貼。

■**Allowance for the Survivor 高齡遺孀津貼：**

若是配偶已過世，則遺孀可以領取此筆津貼。

■**CPP(Canada Pension Plan) 加拿大退休金計劃：**

過去在加拿大工作期間有存款進此退休金帳戶，即可在滿65歲時提領。

■**RPP(Registered Pension Plan) 退休基金計劃：**

由僱主提供的退休基金計劃。

參、其他福利：

■**Home Buyers Plan 首次購屋計劃：**

每個申請人可以從他的RRSP中提取一筆金額做為購屋基金，並於15年內分期償還給RRSP，則此筆款項可以不作為收入提報。

■**Government Housing 政府住宅：**

為了保證人者有其屋，保證低收入者也能住房，加拿大政府每年都撥款建造大批的政府房，由政府委託的專門公司管理，以極低的價格出租。

■**TSFA(Tax Free Savings Account) 免稅儲蓄帳戶：**

凡滿18歲以上加拿大居民，都可於財務機構開設免稅儲蓄帳戶，帳戶內利息收入不會列入應納稅額的收入。

Tips

　　凡滿18歲以上加拿大居民，都可於財務機構開設免稅儲蓄帳戶，每年每人可存入$6,000(2021年TSFA存款限額)，每年限額會依通貨膨脹指數調整，帳戶內利息收入不會列入應納稅額的收入。

　　若是某年沒有存入最高限額，則餘額可加在未來存款限額使用；若是提款後，提款額度也可加在未來存款限額使用，但是只能加在下一年度的存款限額，否則當年度可能會有每月1%的超額罰款。

■**GIS(Guaranteed Income Supplement) 保證收入津貼：**
加拿大政府針對領有OAS老年保障的居民，並且提供額外低收補助。

■**Healthcare Plan 醫療保健計劃：**
除牙科和眼科外，病人看醫生，不須支付診金、化驗費、住院和手術等費用，只須支付處方類藥費。

■**失業金：**
加拿大政府對公民或永久居民在失業後，提供的暫時經濟資助。

■**Vacation Opportunity 帶薪休假：**
加拿大政府規定：全職僱員在工作一年後可獲每年兩週（十個工作日）有薪假期；連續工作五年後，可獲每年三周有薪假期。

■懷孕及育兒津貼：

懷孕津貼只發給親生母親，最長15個星期。育兒津貼是給予孩子的親生或領養父母，最長10個星期。親生母親可同時申請懷孕及育兒津貼。

除了上面所說的福利之外，加拿大是世界上教育體系最完善、教育水準最高的國家之一。公立學校從幼兒園到高中實行完全免費的義務教育，高等教育水平也在全世界名列前茅，擁有數所世界一流學校。

第二章

移民前
稅制規劃

　　不論定居加拿大的原因是什麼，移民到新的國度都是非常不簡單的，有可能需要花費大把金錢及時間才能達成，當一切準備就緒後，在前往加拿大前有些事情是必須先做好規劃的，其中大家最關心的便是關於海外收入及資產方面的稅務問題了，事先在入境加拿大前將資產做好完善規劃，可以避免入境後增加額外的稅金損失。

第一節 入境前資產配置規劃

　　對於計畫來加拿大定居生活的新移民，在身份獲准以後，入境加拿大之前在稅務上應該做哪些準備工作呢？不管是從財務還是稅務上來說，入境前的一個重要準備工作就是要替海外資產彙整一份清單，包括：現金存款、不動產、股票、債權和基金等等。

壹、入境前資產處置：

　　列好詳細海外資產清單後，還需準備收集好相關證明，若是需要公證單位驗證或是專業評估也須及早準備，以證明資產的存在及價值。

一、資產價值證明：

這些準備主要有3個目的：

1.移民後合法轉移資金到加拿大

➡加拿大以外的收入，如薪資、退休金及利息等等，盡量在未移民前全數收取，因為移民前的海外收入，是不會被列入加拿大政府的課稅範圍的。

➡在加拿大以外的投資，若是獨資或合夥行號，因為營業淨利會併入個人收入，日後會有被課徵海外收入的問題，最好是以有限公司的模式經營及參與投資，若是公司不分配盈餘，則可以避免加拿大的股息收入所得稅。另外也建議退出公司董事，那麼海外公司盈利便可避免被加拿大政府徵稅，惟仍需注意CFC(Controlled Foreign Corporation)受控外國企業制度及FAPI(Foreign Accrual Property Income)海外受控公司被動投資所得的相關規定。

2.作為海外資產申報的依據

➡移民前首先要將所有加拿大以外的資產做估價。當移民成為加拿大公民，政府會視所有資產都在移民當日購入，以當時價值做為日後資產增值稅計算基準。

3.方便資本增值稅計算

➡ 大部分新移民在成為加拿大居民後，會繼續持有移民前擁有的海外資產。在申報海外資產時，對於這些資產成本的計算，按照成為加拿大居民那一天的市場價值來計算。好處是，移民前所積累的資本增值部分無需在加拿大交稅。因此，為了便於日後申報海外資產，應收集證明作為申報海外資產的依據。

二、成本提升法 (Step-up in the cost base)：

在移民加拿大前，建議透過「成本提升法」，將個人資產盡量提升到市場價值，因為在入境的第一天成為加拿大稅務居民時，會被視為出售所有資產及重新購入所有資產，若是沒有將個人資產成本提升的話，會造成以原購買成本計算增值額度，而在加拿大居住期間，資產的增值越多，須繳納的資本利得稅就越多。

三、海外持有不動產：

移民前首先要將所有加拿大境外的財產作估價，如果要對不動產進行買賣或移轉，建議要在入境前辦理完成。當入境加拿大成為稅務居民後，加拿大政府會視所有資產都在移民當日購入。假設日後交易不動產，應課稅收入計算方式會以成交價減去入境當日的不動產市價，來計算不動產交易應課稅獲利，舉例來說，假設你在台灣有一間房屋，當初以台幣500萬購入，入境加拿大時當日市價台幣700萬，日後出售價格台幣800萬元，則應課稅交易收入只會計算賺取的台幣100萬收入。

若是位於海外的不動產屬於自住用途，加拿大居民可享有一間自住不動產（Principal Residence）免稅優惠，全球各地的不動產皆適用，但是僅限1間，此間自住用途的不動產進行交易時，即使出售有獲利，該不動產仍不用課稅。

貳、海外資產申報：

新移民最關心的便是海外資產課稅問題，那到底哪些人需要申報海外資產呢?申報海外資產其實不需要繳納額外的稅金，只是要向加拿大政府說明您在海外有多少資產，依照ITA(Income Tax Act) **所得稅法**只有在資產產生海外收入或是出售獲利時才需要課徵所得稅或是資產增值稅。

Tips

ITA(Income Tax Act) 所得稅法

　　為使加拿大居民確實填報其海內外收入，加拿大政府發表的「ITA (Income Tax Act)所得稅法」於1996年1月1日生效，要求加拿大居民有以下四種情形之一都須填報海外收入：

一、海外資產總額超過$100,000

➡包括海外流動資金、海外不動產、海外證卷所股票、海外受控公司股票等等

二、持有海外公司股份

➡擁有至少1%股權，及連同親屬共同持有10%以上股權

三、接收海外信託收益或信託資本分配或貸款

四、海外不動產交易(直接或間接)或貸款海外信託

一、申報對象：

　　在成為稅務居民後，第一次報稅不需要申報海外資產。主要是由於加拿大稅務局考慮到新移民剛來到加拿大，需要一定的時間來適應新的環境和了解相關的稅務申報要求，但從第二次申報個人所得稅開始後的每年都要申報。在第二次報稅起，如果您在加拿大以外地區擁有超過 $100,000的總資產，包括存款、股票、債權、信託投資及房地產等等，則需要於每年報稅時一併遞交

T1135表格向加拿大政府申報海外資產。

[T1135申報豁免]如下述項目在加拿大境外總資產超過 $100,000，亦無須在T1135表格中填報：

■自用的財產，例如自住用途的房屋、自用的汽車等等，用於自己或是父母親友居住的房子是不用在T1135表上申報的。但是不申報，不等於不用納稅。加拿大稅務局規定，每對夫妻在全球有一套自住房的增值稅是可以免稅的，這套房叫做你的「主要住宅」。雖然不需申報海外資產，但是若出售有獲利的部分還是需要列報收入。

■持有加拿大境外公司股份，總價值不超過 $100,000則不需申報海外資產。若是超過則須要填報T1134表格中報海外附屬企業。

■個人消費性資產不需申報，跟自住用途房產同理，因為無法給你帶來任何收入，因此不用申報，例如：珠寶、首飾、相機等等。

■公司資產不需申報，例如：公司名下的機器、廠房、土地等等，因為那是公司資產，就算那些房產有產生租金等收入也是公司收入，不應該計入您個人的收入。

如果您在加拿大以外的國家或地區擁有附屬企業超過10%以上的股份，那麼就需要向加拿大稅務局申報海外附屬企業，新移民第一次報稅時並不需要申報，但是須於稅務年度第二年結束後10

個月內申報海外附屬企業。對於申報人來說，很多人只申報自己個人的海外資產而不申報海外附屬企業，他們會認為公司的資產不屬於個人，不應該納入個人財產申報，但是海外附屬企業不用填報T1135表格，應該要填報T1134表格，若是隱瞞海外附屬企業，會對未來收入轉入加拿大造成影響，還可能被懷疑逃漏稅並加以罰款。

[T1134申報豁免]若是海外附屬企業符合以下條件之一，則不需申報：

■投資成本不超過 $100,000且處於停業狀態，企業總資產不超過 $1,000,000
■企業年收入少於 $25,000

二、計算資產價值：

　　加拿大境外資產計算價值時，會以市場價值來計算，通常是以成為加拿大的稅務居民當天計算 ，一般是入境當天，計算海外資產的「公平市場價值」，即當天的市價加上其他相關雜費。舉例來說：你2022年8月11日入境加拿大成為新移民，海外資產總額便是以2022年8月11日這天的市場價格為基準，新移民的第一個稅務年度不需申報海外資產，因此2023年4月30日前不用填報

T1135表格，要到2024年4月30日前才需填報T1135表格申報海外資產，如果海外資產沒有經過交易，那麼每年的海外資產就一直申報入境當天的市場價值即可。

　　只有在海外資產進行交易出售時，才會按當時的匯率折算加幣計算獲利或虧損，並填報在當年度個人收入。房產，非上市公司股份等要找第三方的評估公司評估，因此在移民前最重要的便是收集資產相關憑證，以利加拿大稅務局查詢，才能在入境後順利將資產提升成本，藉此降低日後出售時所需課徵的個人所得稅。

以下是常見海外資產類別及相關交易憑證：

1.不動產➡當天市價，加上購入不動產時的其他費用。

　　文件包括有關不動產的以下資訊：

　　✓ 建物權狀

　　✓ 謄本

　　✓ 房屋稅單

　　✓ 買賣交易文件

　　✓ 付款證明

2.股票➡當天的收盤價，加上買入股票時的手續費。

　　文件包括持有股票的以下資訊：

　　✓ 證券商開戶文件

✓ 歷史交易記錄

✓ 入境前市值證明

3. 現金➡主要是銀行存款，以當天的加幣匯率換算至加幣。

能證明資金的證明包括以下文件：

✓ 銀行對帳單

✓ 月結單

✓ 存款證明

✓ 銀行帳戶開戶文件

4. 股份➡持有股份證明書是持有公司股份資產的證據。

文件包括持有股份的以下資訊：

✓ 持有股份證明書

✓ 買賣交易文件

✓ 投資協議

✓ 付款證明

5. 基金➡當天的市價，加上買入基金時的手續費。

文件包括有關基金的以下資訊：

✓ 投資的開戶文件

✓ 歷史交易記錄

✓ 入境前市值

6.債務➡包括借據、應收款、帳款、債券等。證明海外債權，首先需證明借貸關係的存在。

文件包括有關借款的以下資訊：

✓ 借款金額

✓ 協議利息

✓ 應償還日期

✓ 借款條件

✓ 債務人償還部分本金或支付利息的證明文件

✓ 借款原因

✓ 債權人如何取得借款的證明文件，例如：轉帳證明

三、申報日期：

新移民在入境後的第一次報稅無須申報海外資產，第二次報稅時，只要總資產超過 $100,000就需於4月30日前申報海外資產。海外資產申報不代表需要繳稅，稅金是依照個人年度所得去計算，資產則是出售時才會計入損益。

新移民第一次報稅時也不需要申報海外附屬企業，但是須於稅務年度第二年結束後10個月內申報海外附屬企業，舉例來說：新移民於2021年7月入境加拿大長久居住，稅務年度的第二年是指2022年1月~12月，則須於2023年10月底前申報海外附屬企業。

四、申報罰則：

若是沒有在4月30日前完成海外資產申報：

申報種類	海外資產總額超過 $100,000	海外附屬企業
表格	T1135	T1134
罰款(1) **逾期未申報**	晚一天罰金 $25，最少 $100，最多逾期100天，亦即上限 $2500。	
罰款(2) **故意逾期未申報而** **稅務局未追討前**	晚一個月罰金 $500，最多晚24個月，上限 $12,000。	
罰款(3) **故意逾期未申報而** **稅務局已發追討書**	罰金提高為每月 $1,000，最多晚24個月，上限 $24,000。	
罰款(4) **逾期申報** **超過24個月**	罰金為所持有海外總資產的5%，再減去上述已繳罰金。	海外附屬企業股票或貸款的5%，再減去上述已繳罰金。
罰款(5) **故意提供不實** **或缺漏資料**	罰金為所持有海外總資產的5%，最少 $24,000。	海外附屬企業股票或貸款的5%，最少 $24,000。

上述提及的故意漏報，如果申報人已積極收集相關資料，但是在資料不齊全的情況下仍準時申報，則不用受罰。

五、表格介紹：

1.T1135表格(申報海外資產)

在2015年後，為簡化海外資產申報報告，當海外資產總金額多於$100,000，但是不超過$250,000時，僅需填報T1135表格的A部分。

表格A部分需填報資料：

✓ 海外資產種類(基金、債務、信託、不動產等等)

✓ 海外資產金額最高前三名國家

✓ 海外資產總收入

✓ 海外資產損益

Part A: Simplified reporting method

For each type of property that applies to you, tick the appropriate box.

Type of property:

Funds held outside Canada .... ☐

Shares of non-resident corporations (other than foreign affiliates) .... ☐

Indebtedness owed by non-resident .... ☐

Interests in non-resident trusts .... ☐

Real property outside Canada (other than personal use and real estate used in an active business) .... ☐

Other property outside Canada .... ☐

Property held in an account with a Canadian registered securities dealer or a Canadian trust company...... ☐

Country code:

Select the top three countries based on the maximum cost amount of specified foreign property held during the year. Enter the country codes in the boxes below:

☐ ☐ ☐

Gross income from all specified foreign property $ _____

Gain(loss) from the disposition from all specified foreign property $ _____

Privacy Act, personal information bank number CRA PPU 035

當海外資產總金額多於$250,000，不僅須填報T1135表格的A部分，B部分也須確實填報，B部分裡面列出來的海外資產主要包括以下七個類別：

(1) 在加拿大境外持有的資金 Funds held outside Canada

- ✓ 基金銀行名稱　　　✓ 國家
- ✓ 持有最高金額　　　✓ 年底持有金額
- ✓ 總收入

1. Funds held outside Canada

Name of bank/other entity holding the funds	Country code	Maximum funds held during the year	Funds held at year-end	Gross income
		Total		

(2)在加拿大境外持有的公司股份 Shares of non-resident corporations

- ✓ 公司名稱　　　✓ 國家
- ✓ 持有最高價值　　　✓ 年底持有市價
- ✓ 總收入　　　✓ 獲利或虧損金額

2. Shares of non-resident corporations (other than foreign affiliates)

Name of corporation	Country code	Maximum cost amount during the year	Cost amount at year-end	Gross Income	Gain (loss) on disposition
		Total			

(3)在加拿大境外持有的債務 Indebtedness owed by non-resident

- ✓ 負債明細　　　✓ 國家
- ✓ 持有最高金額　　　✓ 年底持有價值
- ✓ 總收入　　　✓ 獲利或虧損金額

3. Indebtedness owed by non-resident

Description of indebtedness	Country code	Maximum cost amount during the year	Cost amount at year-end	Gross Income	Gain (loss) on disposition
		Total			

(4)在加拿大境外持有的信託權益Interests in non-resident trusts

✓ 信託名稱　　　　　　　✓ 國家

✓ 持有最高金額　　　　　✓ 年底持有金額

✓ 收入　　　　　　　　　✓ 收到信託資金

✓ 獲利或虧損金額

4. Interests in non-resident trusts

Name of Trust	Country code	Maximum cost amount during the year	Cost amount at year-end	Income received	Capital received	Gain (loss) on disposition
		Total				

(5)加拿大境外的房地產(自住除外) Real property outside Canada

✓ 房地產說明　　　　　　✓ 國家

✓ 持有最高市價　　　　　✓ 年底持有市價

✓ 總收入　　　　　　　　✓ 獲利或虧損金額

5. Real property outside Canada (other than personal use and real estate used in an active business)

Description of property	Country code	Maximum cost amount during the year	Cost amount at year-end	Gross income	Gain (loss) on disposition
		Total			

(6)加拿大境外的其他財產 Other property outside Canada

✓ 財產說明 ✓ 國家

✓ 持有最高市價 ✓ 年底持有市價

✓ 總收入 ✓ 獲利或虧損金額

6. Other property outside Canada

Description of property	Country code	Maximum cost amount during the year	Cost amount at year-end	Gross income	Gain (loss) on disposition
		Total			

(7)持有在加拿大註冊的證券商或加拿大信託公司帳戶內持有的財產 Property held in an account with a Canadian registered securities dealer or a Canadian trust company

✓ 證券商或信託公司名稱

✓ 國家

✓ 持有最高市場公允價值

✓ 年底持有市場公允價值

✓ 總收入

✓ 獲利或虧損金額

7. Property held in an account with a Canadian registered securities dealer or a Canadian trust company

Name of registered security dealer/Canadian trust company	Country code	Maximum fair market value during the year	Fair market value at year-end	Gross income	Gain (loss) on disposition
		Total			

2.T1134表格(申報海外附屬企業)

如果您在加拿大以外的國家或地區擁有附屬企業超過10%以上的股份,那麼就需要向加拿大稅務局申報海外附屬企業,新移民第一次報稅時並不需要申報,但是須於稅務年度第二年結束後10個月內填報T1134表格申報海外附屬企業。如果是2020年的表格則需於稅務年度第二年結束後12個月內申報。

T1134表格需填報資料:

✓ 持有海外附屬公司數量　　✓ 公司所在地

✓ 公司資木額　　　　　　　✓ 持股比例

✓ 主要營業項日　　　　　　✓ 午度進出口額度

✓ 公司營運規模　　　　　　✓ 主要股東及股權比例

若是海外附屬企業符合以下條件之一,則不需申報:

1.投資成本不超過 $100,000且處於停業狀態,企業總資產不超過 $1,000,000

2.企業年收入少於 $25,000

Protected B when completed

Canada Revenue   Agence du revenu
Agency   du Canada

Information Return Relating to Controlled and Non-Controlled Foreign Affiliates
(2021 and later taxation years)
T1134 Summary Form

Do not use this area

- Use this version of the return for taxation years that begin after 2020.
- For T1134 returns that are filed in respect of taxation years that begin before 2021, please use the previous version of the T1134 form as released on November 28, 2017.
- For any amended T1134 return, please use the same version as the original T1134 return filed.
- Refer to the instructions before you complete the T1134 Summary and Supplements.
- A separate supplement must be filed for each foreign affiliate. However, do not file a supplement for a "dormant" or "inactive" foreign affiliate.
- Refer to the instructions for the definition of dormant or inactive foreign affiliates.
- References on this return to the foreign affiliate or the affiliate refer to the foreign affiliate for which the reporting entity is filing a supplement.
- If you are reporting on a partnership, references to year or taxation year should be read as fiscal period.
- If you need more space to report information, you can use attachments.
- If an election has been made to use functional currency, state the alphabetic currency code of the functional currency. (Note: only certain corporations can elect to report in a functional currency - see instructions.) . . . .

If this is an amended return, tick this box. ☐

Is this T1134 Summary filed for one reporting entity or a group of reporting entities that are related to each other? (see instructions)

☐ One reporting entity   ☐ A group of reporting entities that are related to each other

If this T1134 Summary is filed for a group of reporting entities that are related to each other, indicate which entity is the representative reporting entity for the related group in Section 1 – reporting entity information.

Part I – Identification
Section 1 – Reporting entity information

Tick a box to indicate who you are reporting for, and complete the areas that apply (please print)

	First name	Last name	Initial(s)	Social insurance number (SIN)
☐ Individual				

	Corporation's name	Business number (BN)		R C	
☐ Corporation					

	Trust's name	Trust's account number		
☐ Trust		T	–	–

	Partnership's name	Partnership's account number		R Z		Partnership Code
☐ Partnership						

Reporting entity's address

Number		Street		
	City	Province/territory or state	Postal or ZIP code	Country code

Reporting entity's NAICS code(s) (6 digits)   1. ____   2. ____   3. ____   4. ____

	Year	Month	Day		Year	Month	Day
For what taxation year are you filing this form? From				To			

Does this period include 2 or more short taxation years? (see instructions)   Yes ☐   No ☐

Number of supplements attached ____

Section 2 – Certification

Person to contact for more information (please print)

First name	Last name	Telephone number

I, _____ , certify that the information given on these T1134 Summary and Supplements are, to the best of my knowledge,
(Print name)
correct and complete.

Date	Authorized signing officer's, or representative's signature	Position, title, officer's rank

第二節 入境後
海外收入規劃

壹、海外收入種類：

移民不代表要放棄原有國家的一切事業，在入境加拿人之後，若是原有國家有收入的話，該怎麼處理呢？

一般來說海外收入主要分為以下四項：

一、薪資收入

二、利息收入

三、投資收入

FAPI(Foreign Accrual Property Income) 海外受控公司被動投資所得

 Tips

有許多加拿大居民透過將資產投資於海外受控公司來規避加拿大所得稅，因為加拿大稅制規定海外受控公司只要沒有登記在加拿大，或是由加拿大居民管理控制就不在加拿大課稅範圍內，為了打擊加拿大納稅人逃漏稅行為，特別設立FAPI條例。

FAPI條例規定，凡加拿大居民獨資或合夥擁有海外受控公司

50%以上控制權，皆須在稅單內填報其在海外受控公司所佔比例的投資收入，所有合夥人中是加拿大居民的合計比例超過50%也需填報，超過四人則不在此限。

FAPI主要是被動的投資收入，包括租金收入、專利權收入、利息等等，假設投資企業僱用五人以上的全職員工，其營業淨收入就不算進FAPI中。

四、資產增值收入

在成為加拿大稅務居民後，如有以下原因需繳交資產增值稅：

1.出售海外資產而產生之收入

➡扣除雜費及成本後繳交資產增值稅。雜費包括契稅、印花稅、產權移轉登記規費、貸款設定規費、履約保證專戶費用、代書費、仲介費等等，舉例來說，買賣1000萬的房產約需要多支出20多萬元的雜費。

2.海外資產相關收入

➡須扣除免稅額後繳交資產增值稅。若是出售海外資產造成的損失，則可以抵銷過去3年的資產增值稅。舉例來說：若是今年出售房產造成損失，如過去3年曾繳交資產增值稅，則可以要求退稅，或是留做未來的資產增值稅扣抵。

貳、收入移轉加拿大：

一、轉入海外資產

　　加拿大稅務局要求稅務居民申報海外資產，是為了避免你日後隱瞞海外收入而逃漏稅，作為加拿大稅務居民，從入境那天起全球收入都須課稅便是你的責任及義務，但是海外資產也不是申報越多越好，雖然申報過的海外資產在未來轉入加拿大時會更加方便，但是要注意的是，申報資產數量規模必須跟未來海外資產產生之收入成合理的比例才行，加拿大稅務局不對稅務居民的海外資產繳稅，但是會對這些海外資產所產生的收入繳稅。

　　若是申報海外收入時，收益跟資產數量嚴重不合理，稅務局就可以合理懷疑是否有漏報海外收入的嫌疑，舉例來說：正常情況來說價值兩千萬的定存存款能產生每年3%約60萬的利息收入，但是申報人只申報10萬元利息收入，明顯不符合比例原則，就容易引起稅務局關注並查稅。

　　既然資產不是申報越多越好，那什麼樣的海外資產是可以安全轉入加拿大的呢？記住海外資產申報的重點不是資產，而是由資產而產生的收入。資產與收入應該有一個比較合理的比例關係。所以，如果你能證明你轉過來的這筆錢是出自以下3個來源，這筆資產就是安全的：

1.移民加拿大前就擁有的現金存款

2.移民以後賺取的收入，並且已確實申報繳稅

3.接受贈與或繼承所獲得的財產

二、海外收入轉入時機

海外收入轉入的時機不同也會有影響，首先建議將預計轉入的現金盡快轉入加拿大，因為在新移民入境的前兩年，加拿大稅務局知道你需要轉入大筆資金安家或是購買房產，因此他們對你資金的轉入審查相對來說會比較寬鬆。不過，如果你正確地申報了海外資產和海外收入，並且做好了充分的準備，任何時候你都可以將資產安全地轉移到加拿大來。

已經申報了的海外資產轉入加拿大的時候的確會比較方便。但是並不意味著您轉入的錢都可以被默認為是您的海外資產。所以當轉帳的時候，還是記得要留下憑據，比如銀行轉帳單。如果是贈與的最好有書面證明。否則真的遇到審查，很可能還是說不清楚資金來源。

三、避免所得稅雙重課稅及防杜逃稅協議

為避免所得稅雙重課稅及防杜逃稅協議(以下簡稱臺加租稅協議)於106年1月1日生效，有助臺加雙方經貿投資往來，提升我國投資

環境吸引力及我商競爭力，進一步深化雙方產業合作與技術交流。

　　臺加租稅協議共28條，主要由所得來源國(例如我國)就他方締約國(例如加拿大)居住者(含人民及企業)取得之各類所得提供合宜之減免稅措施，以消除重複課稅，甚至減輕稅負，並提供爭議解決機制，主要內容如下：

適用對象	一、居住者：指符合我國或加拿大各自稅法規定之居住者，包括個人及企業。 二、雙重居住者： (一)個人：依序考量其永久住所、主要利益中心、經常居所，或相互協議決定其唯一居住者身分。 (二)企業：相互協議決定
適用稅目	所得稅
營業利潤	我國或加拿人企業於對方國家從事營業未構成「常設機構(以下簡稱PE)」，其「營業利潤」免稅。PE包括： (一)固定PE：例如管理處、分支機構、辦事處等。 (二)工程PE：工程存續期間超過6個月。 (三)服務PE：提供服務天數於任何12個月期間合計超過183天。 (四)代理人PE：代表一國企業之人，有權代表該企業在對方國家簽訂契約，並經常行使該權力。 但在對方國家設立之固定營業場所(例如發貨倉庫)僅從事該企業貨物之儲存、展示或運送、專為該企業採購貨物、商品或蒐集資訊等具有準備或輔助性質活動者，不視為PE。

投資所得	一、股利：公司直接或間接持股20%以上，上限稅率10%；其他情況上限稅率15%。 二、利息：上限稅率10%；特定利息免稅。 三、權利金：上限稅率10%。
財產交易所得	一、股份交易所得原則免稅。 二、提供已課徵離境稅之財產消除重複課稅之規定。

　　此外，我國人退休後移居加國成為加國居住者取得我國養老金所得，我國稅法排除於課稅所得之外部分(例如退職所得定額免稅)，加國亦應免稅。旅加華僑日後回流臺灣，出售財產之所得，屬於移出加拿大時已課徵加拿大離境稅之所得部分，可排除於我國課稅範圍之外。

第三章

加拿大
個人稅務

加拿大身為「萬稅之國」，課稅方式及福利制度都非常多樣化，更有多種節稅管道。聯邦和省政府有各自的稅收管轄權。加拿大的稅務居民需分別繳納聯邦稅和地方稅。聯邦政府透過加拿大國家稅務局（Canada Revenue Agency）對聯邦和地方個人所得稅進行課徵。聯邦稅中適用於個人稅的部分主要為：聯邦所得和資本利得稅、商品和服務稅（增值稅的一種）和社會保險稅。目前加拿大並未開徵遺產稅和贈與稅，但是當稅務居民死亡或發生贈與時，可能會被視同資本利得而課徵資本利得稅。地方稅中適用於個人稅的部分主要為：地方所得和資本利得稅以及商品和服務稅。

 # 第一節 所得稅

加拿大的稅務年度跟台灣一樣是歷年制，每年1月1日到12月31日止，納稅年度終了後，需於隔年4月30日前申報上一年度的所得稅，對於自僱的納稅人，則截止期限到隔年的6月15日前。在魁北克省以外的省及地區，個人僅需準備一份包含聯邦稅及地方稅的申報表格，若是在魁北克省，則必須分別申報聯邦稅和地方稅。

如果逾期申報會有5%的滯報金罰款，另加徵每月1%的滯納金，上限12個月。除了每年4月30日前須申報所得稅並繳納稅金以外，加拿大亦有暫繳稅金制度，金額以去年收入為基準，分四個季度暫繳，分別在3月15日、6月15日、9月15日、12月15日。應繳納金額少於$3,000則不需要預繳稅金。加拿大是以個人為單位進行所得稅申報而不是以家庭為單位申報，主要原因是為了防止高收入的家庭成員透過低收入的家庭成員來享受較低的所得稅率。計算稅額時，申報人可以根據自身情況適用各類扣除額、免稅項目及稅收抵免項目，以下將針對加拿大個人稅制作詳細介紹。

壹、納稅義務人：

一、永久居住在加拿大：

1.加拿大居民：

　　永久居住在加拿大生活和工作的加拿大居民，申報所得稅不僅有機會取得稅金減免，大多福利津貼都會要求報稅紀錄作為申請標準，例如：加拿大工人福利（CWB）、加拿大兒童福利金（CCB）、商品和服務稅/統一銷售稅（GST/ HST)抵免、保證收入補助（GIS）；若是有配偶或同居伴侶也需要申報，除此之外，符合以下條件都需要申報所得稅：

■您和配偶或同居伴侶選擇分割養老金收入

■您在當年買賣或出租不動產

■您必須償還全部或部分老人年金(OAS)福利、就業保險 (EI) 福利或加拿大康復福利（CRB）

■您尚未償還首次購屋計劃（HBP）或終身學習計劃（LLP)從冊退休儲蓄計劃（RRSP）中提取的所有金額

■您必須為 2021 年的加拿大退休金計劃（CPP)存款

■您正在為自僱收入支付就業保險（EI）保費

■您想轉移未使用的學費或將未使用的學費、教育和教科書金額結轉到未來一年

■您希望申報的收入可以讓您向註冊退休儲蓄計劃（RRSP）、養老金計劃（PRPP)或指定養老金計劃（SPP）存款

■您想要申報收入，以增加您的加拿大信用額度。

2.加拿大新移民：

　　加拿大身為移民熱門國家，每年入境的新移民數量非常多，這些移民到加拿大定居的新移民們，最想知道的是加拿大以高稅收高福利聞名，那福利津貼該怎麼領取呢？ 稅收又該如何申報呢？當你在加拿大有長期住所，你就成為加拿大的所得稅居民，舉例來說：獲得永居身分、透過合法簽證留在加拿大等等，只有成為

加拿大新居民的第一個納稅年度適用。在加拿大的第一個納稅年度之後，您不再被視為所得稅的新移民。

▶申請津貼資格

　　在加拿大要獲得這些福利，您或您的配偶或同居伴侶必須是永久居民，並在獲得社會保險號碼後立即申請福利，如果您是臨時居民，您必須在加拿大連續居住18 個月 ，並在您在加拿大居住的第 19 個月持有有效許可證，然後才能申請加拿大兒童福利和任何相關的計劃。

	已婚或同居有孩子	單身有孩子	已婚或同居無孩子	單身且年滿19歲無孩子
加拿大兒童福利	V	V	X	X
商品和服務稅/統一銷售稅(GST/HST)抵免	V	V	V	V

　　在申請福利津貼後，即使你當年無收入，您每年還是都需要按時提交您的所得稅即獲得福利申報表，配偶或同居伴侶也需要每年申報。

▶收入來源

新移民申報所得稅收入來源分為兩階段，第一階段是入境的第一個稅務年度，需要申報以下收入：

■在加拿大的薪資或在加拿大經營業務的營業收入

■買賣或出租加拿大財產的應課稅資本收益

■您從加拿大獲得的獎學金、助學金、研究金和研究補助金的應課稅部分

第二階段是入境後第二個稅務年度，在你被視為加拿大居民的稅務年度，你需要申報全世界的收入，意指在加拿大境內境外的所有收入，若是來自加拿大境外的養老金收入，根據稅收協定可能免稅，但是仍需要在申報表上申報該收入，例如：台灣人退休後移居加國成為加國居住者取得中華民國養老金所得，我國稅法排除於課稅所得之外部分(例如退職所得定額免稅)，加國亦應免稅。

▶入境前取得之財產

如果你在入境加拿大前持有房產，加拿大稅務局會認定你在入境當日已出售這些房產，並立即以當日公允價值的成本重新購回，包括外幣、股票、珠寶、收藏品等等皆是以公允價值方式計算財產價值，因此務必於入境前盡量將所有財產成本提升到公允價值，並收集證明文件及單據以供未來查驗。

如果你因為處置這些財產而遭受損失，您只能從出售同類型財產的任何收益中扣除這些損失。例如：出售A房產損失，可以從B房產獲利中扣除。你不能使用這種類型的損失來減少你從出售其他類型的財產中獲得的任何資本收益。

▶收入扣除額

你可以透過申請符合資格的扣除額來減少你的總收入。總收入減掉扣除額後才是你的應課稅收入，用於計算聯邦稅金和省或地區稅金。以下是常見的扣除額：

■註冊退休儲蓄計劃存款

般來說，如果這是新移民將在加拿人提交申報表的第一年，則你不能在 2021 年扣除您對註冊退休儲蓄計劃 (RRSP) 的存款。

■養老金收入分配

如果你和你的配偶或同居伴侶在 2021 年 12 月 31 日是加拿大居民，你可以選擇分割部分養老金收入給配偶或同居伴侶。

■搬家費用

一般來說，新移民不能扣除移居加拿大所產生的搬家費用。但是，如果您以全日制學生的身份進入加拿大就讀大學、學院或其他教育機構的專科課程，並且您獲得了應納稅的加拿大獎學金、助學金、研究金，或研究補助金進入該教育機構，您可能有資格扣除您的搬家費用。

■撫養費用

如果您支付配偶或子女撫養費,即使您的前配偶或同居伴侶不住在加拿大,您也可以扣除您支付的撫養費金額。

二、暫時居住在加拿大:

1.非加拿大居民:

一般來說,只要您符合以下條件之一就會被認定為非加拿大居民:

■通常居住於加拿大境外,並且未被認定為加拿大居民。

■全年於加拿大境外居住,並且在加拿大沒有長期居住地。

■一年在加拿大居住的天數少於 183 天,並且在加拿大沒有長期居住地。

非加拿大居民還是需要就加拿大境內的收入報稅,依收入來源分為兩種,第一種是以下項目,通常稅率為25%,並且須由付款人於支付款項時先行扣除稅金部分,以下為扣繳申報所得稅的常見項目:

✓ 股利收入　　　　　　　✓ 租金收入

✓ 權利金使用費收入　　　✓ 養老金收入

✓ 老年保障金收入　　　　✓ 加拿大退休金計劃

✓ 領取退休津貼　　　　　✓ 註冊退休儲蓄計劃金

✓ 註冊退休收入基金付款　　✓ 年金

✓ 管理費

　　第二種是以下項目，不事使用扣繳方式申報，須由納稅義務人透過填寫所得稅申報表進行申報：

✓ 加拿大薪資所得

✓ 加拿大做生意所得

✓ 加拿大獎學金、助學金、補助金和研究補助金中應稅的部分

✓ 買賣加拿大資產的資本收益

✓ 在加拿大非全職服務所得

▶ **報稅期限**

　　納稅年度後次年的 4 月 30 日

▶ **兒童福利**

　　作為非居民，您無法獲得加拿大兒童福利金 (CCB)，除非您是被視為居民的配偶或同居伴侶，並且您符合 CCB 的資格要求。

2.被視為居民:

　　您一年在加拿大居住 183 天或更長時間，並且在加拿大沒有長

期居住地。則您被視為加拿大居民,您必須申報整個納稅年度的全球收入(來自加拿大境內外所有的收入),當您計算您在納稅年度期間在加拿大停留的天數時,包括:

■就讀於加拿大大學或學院期間

■在加拿大工作期間

■在加拿大旅遊度假期間

■居住在美國並通勤往返加拿大(通勤時間不計入)

▶納稅義務

✓ 申請扣除額

✓ 申請不可退還的稅收抵免

✓ 繳納聯邦稅

✓ 申請聯邦稅收抵免

✓ 申請商品和服務稅/統一銷售稅 (GST/HST) 抵免

✓ 不能申請省或地區稅收抵免

▶居住過魁北克

若是一年中在加拿大居住滿183天,除了會被視為居民以外,有在魁北克省居住過還可能被視為該省的居民。如果被視為魁北克省的居民,就算您已經不在該省分居住,仍需要繳納魁北克所得稅，為避免雙重課稅，需在申報所得稅時向聯邦稅務局告知以下資訊：

✓ 您是魁北克省的稅務居民

✓ 您正在申報魁北克省所得稅

✓ 您要求免除非居民和被視為加拿大居民的附加稅

▶報稅期限

納稅年度後隔年的 4 月 30 日

▶兒童福利

　　一旦被視為加拿大居民，報稅是應盡的義務，但也同時能享有高福利政策的權利，只要您符合加拿大兒童福利金 (CCB)資格則可以繼續領取，直到離開加拿大為止。如果您在加拿大境外有孩子，您可以通過向 加拿大稅務局CRA 發送填妥的RC66 表格來申請 CCB 。

Canada Revenue   Agence du revenu
Agency   du Canada

Canada Child Benefits Application
includes federal, provincial, and territorial programs

Find out if this form is for you

Fill out this form to apply for the Canada child benefit and register your children for the goods and services tax/harmonized sales tax (GST/HST) credit, the climate action incentive payment (CAIP) and related federal, provincial, or territorial programs the Canada Revenue Agency (CRA) administers. You can also use this form if you started a shared-custody situation for one or more children.

Do not fill out this form if you already applied using My Account on the CRA website or when you registered the birth of your newborn with your province or territory (except Yukon and Nunavut).

Who should fill out this form

The person who is **primarily responsible** for the care and upbringing of the child should apply (see "Primarily responsible for the care and upbringing of the child" on page 3).

When a child resides with a female parent in the home, the female parent is usually considered to be primarily responsible for the child and should apply. However, if the child's other parent is primarily responsible, they should apply and attach a signed letter from the female parent stating that the other parent with whom she resides is primarily responsible for all the children in the home. If the child lives with same-sex parents, only one parent should apply for all the children in the home.

For more information

For more information on the Canada child benefit, including eligibility requirements, go to **canada.ca/cra-benefits**, see Booklet T4114, Canada Child Benefit, or call **1-800-387-1193**. From outside Canada or the United States, call **1-613-940-8495**. We accept collect calls by automated response.

Step 1 – Your information

Social insurance number (SIN):

If you do not have a SIN, see Booklet T4114, Canada Child Benefit, under "How to apply."

First name:

Last name:

Date of birth:
Year   Month   Day

Your language of correspondence: ☐ English   ☐ Français

Phone numbers: Home: Work: Ext: Cell:

Step 2 – Your address

Mailing address

Apt. No. – Street No., Street name, PO Box, RR:

City:

Province or territory (or country if outside Canada):

Postal or ZIP code:

Have you moved from a different province or territory within the last 12 months?   ☐ Yes   ☐ No

If **yes**, enter the previous province or territory and the date you moved: Date: Year   Month   Day

Home address   ☐ Same as mailing address

Apt. No. – Street No., Street name, RR:

City:

Province or territory (or country if outside Canada):

Postal or ZIP code:

Canada

3.國際學生：

　　如果您是在加拿大讀書的國際學生，您也可能需要申報所得稅，首先需要確定您的居留身分，並透過該身份別的申報方式申報所得稅，一般來說加拿大留學生會是以下四種居留身份之一：

■居民：有加拿大長期住所、新移民、有駕照信用卡健康保險等等。

■非居民：在加拿大沒有長期住所，但是一年中居住滿183天。

■被視為居民：在加拿大沒有長期住所，但是一年中居住滿183天，並且不被視為原國籍的稅務居民。

■被視為非居民：在加拿大有長期住所，但是被另一個國家視為稅務居民，則會被加拿大視為非居民。

貳、收入種類：

　　加拿大執行的是「自動申報」報稅制度，納稅人有責任向稅務局申報所有收入，並自行計算稅金。加拿大需要申報的所得大致可以分為以下九類：薪資所得、雇傭所得、自雇所得、投資所得、生意所得、資本所得、海外受控公司投資所得、養老和儲蓄計劃所得、福利所得。各類所得的具體範圍如下：

一、應課稅收入：

▶Employment Income 薪資所得：

在加拿大境內或海外透過工作獲取的薪資收入，包括獎金、加給津貼、小費等等，須列入薪資所得，以下不計入薪資所得：

- ✓ 取得工作用手機
- ✓ 同工作非自願搬遷(40哩以上)的搬家費用、換屋的佣金、稅金、裝修等等公司補貼金
- ✓ 生日節慶禮金，限2件且總價不超過$500
- ✓ 工作獎勵，限2件且總價不超過$500
- ✓ 電腦、學習課程、制服等等

▶其他雇傭所得：

其他未在T4報稅單上申報的收入，例如：研究經費淨所得、神職人員住房補貼或、收入維持保險計劃（薪資損失補償計劃）所得、退伍軍人福利、特定的GST/HST和魁北克銷售稅返還、特許權使用費、從補充失業福利計劃取得的金額、人壽保險計劃繳費相關的應稅福利、員工利潤分享計劃、醫療保險福利、工薪收入者保障計劃等等，

▶自雇所得：

透過提供專業服務之傭金、經營農業漁業等收入。

▶Inrestment Income 投資所得：

透過財產而獲取的收入，不論是從加拿大應稅企業取得股息或是海外利息，包括利息、股利、房產淨租金等等，都應列入投資所得。自住房屋出租如利用Airbnb等則不認列，同理若出租有虧損也不得抵減稅金，另外加拿大稅制有針對股利收入給予優惠(Dividend Tax Credit)，發股利的公司先繳過所得稅後才發股利，因此，實際上是以較低的稅率去補償公司已付的公司所得稅。

▶Business Income 生意所得：

不論是獨資或合夥，透過經商做生意的營運收入，須列入生意所得。類似台灣的行號模式，營業收入併入個人年度所得計算。

▶Capital Gains 資本所得：

企業營運收入以外與企業資本相關收入，例如:出售固定資產所獲取的收入，應列入資本所得。是以出售的價格減去成本來計算收益，以淨收入的50%計算資本所得。但是賭博性質獲利不計入收入，若有虧損亦不得要求稅金抵減。

▶**FAPI(Foreign Accrual Property Income) 海外受控公司被動投資所得：**

獨資或合夥擁有海外受控公司50%以上控制權，皆須在稅單內填報其在海外受控公司所佔比例的投資收入。(參閱第二章第二節)

> Tips
>
> 舉例來說，適用FAPI例子：
> 1.加拿大居民獨資擁有海外受控公司100%股權
> 2.加拿大居民與外國人合夥擁有海外受控公司，其中加拿大居民持有超過50%股份。
> 3.加拿大居民及其家屬擁有合計超過50%海外受控公司股份
> 4.不超過4位的加拿大居民擁有合計超過50%海外受控公司

以上例子皆須申報該海外受控公司的年度營收，並按持股比例強制計算股東年度所得，無論是否實際分配股利，除非該公司實際雇用5名以上全職員工，證明非紙上公司，則不計入FAPI。

▶**Old age security養老金、Withdrawals from RRSP註冊退休儲蓄計劃所得及Pension Plan退休金：**

1.老年保障養老金所得
2.加拿大養老金計劃和魁北克養老金計劃福利

3. 從海外獲得的退休金

4. 其他養老金或退休金所得

5. 在選擇分配養老金下取得的所得

6. 註冊傷殘儲蓄計劃所得

7. 註冊退休儲蓄計劃所得

8. 一次性給付所得，例如：推出計劃時從養老金和遞延利潤分
   配計劃中獲得的一次性給付所得

9. 退休津貼（遣散費）

10. 聯邦補充所得淨額（在納稅年度內收到的補充保障所得）

▶福利所得：

1. 托兒津貼

2. 就業保險和其他福利

3. 勞工賠償福利

4. 社會援助金

二、不須課稅收入

　　雖然身為加拿大稅務居民，收入如實納稅是居民應盡的義務，
但是也不是所有收入都需要繳納所得稅，基於公益及補償緣故，
以下所得不需要作為收入申報所得稅：

■GST商品和服務稅/HST統一銷售稅

➡任何商品和服務稅/統一銷售稅抵扣額、加拿大兒童福利津貼

或加拿大兒童稅收福利金，包括從相關省計劃獲得的福利。

■魁北克省支付的兒童救助金及殘疾兒童的補充救助金

■由政府向犯罪案件或交通事故受害者提供的補償金

■彩票獎金

■贈與獲得財產

■遺產獲得財產

■因戰爭導致傷殘或死亡而獲得的撫恤金

■透過人壽保險單而獲得的死亡理賠金

■因罷工而從工會取得的收入

■小學及中學獎學金和助學金

■有資格的全日制學生收到的高等教育獎學金、助學金、補助金

■從免稅儲蓄帳戶(TFSA)獲得的款項

　　值得注意的是，因以上不須課稅的收入而取得的收入，需繳納所得稅，例如：遺產取得房產出租的租金收入、彩票獎金存放銀行獲得利息收入等等，皆需要繳納所得稅。

參、稅前扣除額：

　　加拿大跟台灣的稅制一樣會有許多可以列舉扣除的項目，納稅人須根據自身的具體情況，和各稅收抵免項目的適用範圍來確定可適用的稅收抵免項目和扣除額，將已支出費用從收入中扣除，例如：撫養扣除額、教育扣除額等等，可以讓納稅義務人在納稅申報表上申報的扣除、抵免和費用，以幫助減少您必須支付的稅額。以下詳細介紹加拿大各種稅前扣除額：

一、育兒扣除額：
▶托兒費用
　　因為父母工作繁忙或是父母就學中而無法整天照顧幼兒，需委託保母或是托兒機構代為照顧而產生之費用，則可以申報托兒費用，前提是申報托兒費用之孩童必須與您同住，才有資格獲得此筆費用。

▶申請身分
➡如果你是唯一撫養幼兒的人，申請時須填寫T778表格的A部分及B部分。

I✦I Canada Revenue Agency   Agence du revenu du Canada

Protected B when completed

Child Care Expenses Deduction for 2021

Before you fill out this form, read the attached information sheet.

Part A – Total child care expenses

First and **last name** and **date of birth** of all your eligible children, even if you did not pay child care expenses for all of them.

			Year	Month	Day

First name of each eligible child for whom payments were made	Child care expenses paid (read note below)	Name of the child care organization or name and social insurance number of the individual who received the payments	Number of weeks for boarding schools or overnight camps
	+		
	+		
	+		
	+		
Total 67950 =			

Note

The maximum you can claim for expenses that relate to a stay in a boarding school (other than education costs) or an overnight camp (including an overnight sports school) is any of the following amounts:

- **$200 per week** for a child included on line 1 in Part B
- **$275 per week** for a child included on line 2
- **$125 per week** for a child included on line 3

Enter the amount of expenses included above that were incurred in 2021 for a child who was 6 or younger at the end of the year.   67954

Part B – Basic limit for child care expenses

Number of eligible children **born in 2015 or later**, for whom the disability amount cannot be claimed	× **$8,000** =	1
Number of eligible children **born in 2021 or earlier**, for whom the disability amount can be claimed *	× **$11,000** = 67960 +	2
Number of eligible children **born in 2005 to 2014**, (and born in 2004 or earlier, with an impairment in physical or mental function, for whom the disability amount cannot be claimed)	× **$5,000** = +	3
Add lines 1 to 3.	=	4
Enter the amount from **line 67950** in Part A.		5
Enter your **earned income**.	× $\frac{2}{3}$ =	6
Enter the amount from line 4, 5, or 6, **whichever is less**.		7

If you are the person with the higher net income, go to Part C. Leave lines 8 and 9 blank.

Enter the amount that the **other person** with the higher net income deducted on line 21400 of his or her 2021 return.	−	8
Line 7 minus line 8. If you attended school in 2021 and you are the only person making a claim, also go to Part D. Otherwise, enter this amount on line 21400 of your return. **Allowable deduction**	=	9

- Attach Form T2201, Disability Tax Credit Certificate. If this form has already been filed for the child, attach a note to your return showing the name and social insurance number of the person who filed the form and the tax year for which it was filed.

T778 E (21)   (Ce formulaire est disponible en français.)   Page 3 of 4   **Canadä**

➡如果你是可申報托兒費用中收入較高者來申請托兒費用的話，
申請時須額外填寫T778表格的C部分。

Part C – Are you the person with the higher net income?

Fill out this part **and** tick the boxes that apply if, in 2021, **another person** with lower net income was in a situation described below.

Name of person with lower net income	Social insurance number	Net income

☐ **a)** The other person attended school and was enrolled in a **part-time** educational program.

☐ **b)** The other person attended school and was enrolled in a **full-time** educational program.

☐ **c)** The other person was not capable of caring for children because of an impairment in physical or mental function. That person must have been confined for a period of at least two weeks to a bed or wheelchair, or as a patient in a hospital, or other similar institution. Attach a statement from the attending physician certifying this information.

☐ **d)** The other person was not capable of caring for children because of an impairment in physical or mental function, and this situation is likely to continue for an indefinite period. Attach a statement from the attending physician certifying this information.

☐ **e)** The other person was confined to a prison or similar institution for a period of at least two weeks.

☐ **f)** You and your spouse or common-law partner were, due to a breakdown in your relationship, living separate and apart at the end of 2021 and for a period of at least 90 days beginning in 2021, but you reconciled before March 2, 2022.

Enter the amount from line 4 in Part B. _____ × 2.5% = _____ **10**

Multiply the amount on line 10 by the number of **weeks** in 2021 that any of the situations in b) to f) existed. _____ **11**

Multiply the amount on line 10 by the number of **months** in 2021 that the situation in a) existed (other than a month that includes a week used to calculate the amount on line 11). _____ **12**

Line 11 plus line 12. `67980` = _____ **13**

Enter **whichever is less**, the amount from line 7 in Part B or line 13.
If you attended school in 2021, go to Part D.
Otherwise, enter this amount on line 21400 of your return. **Allowable deduction** _____ **14**

➡如果你在申報時同時具備就學身分，申請時須額外填寫T778表格的D部分。

Part D – Were you enrolled in an educational program in 2021?

Fill out this part if, at any time in 2021, either of the following situations applied to you:

- you were the **only person supporting the eligible child**, line 7 equals line 6 in Part B, and you were enrolled in an educational program
- you were the **person with the higher net income**, line 7 equals line 6 in Part B, and, at the same time in 2021, you **and another person** were enrolled in an educational program. **But first, fill out Part C**

Part D does not apply to the person with the lower net income, since the other person will claim this part of the deduction for both of them.

Enter the amount from line 4 in Part B.	$\times$ 2.5% =		15
Multiply the amount on line 15 by the number of **weeks** in 2021 during which you were enrolled in a **full-time** educational program. If there was **another person**, they must also have been enrolled in a **full-time** educational program during the **same weeks**.			16
Multiply the amount on line 15 by the number of **months** (other than any month that includes a week used to calculate the amount on line 16) in 2021 during which one of the following applies:			
• there was no **other person** and you were enrolled in a **part-time** educational program			
• you and the other person were enrolled in a **full-time** or **part-time** educational program during the **same months**	+		17
Line 16 plus line 17		67990 =	18
Line 4 in Part B minus line 9 in Part B or line 14 in Part C, whichever applies to you			19
Line 5 in Part B minus line 9 in Part B or line 14 in Part C, whichever applies to you			20
Enter your **net income** (not including amounts on lines 21400 and 23500).	$\times$ $\frac{2}{3}$ =		21
If you filled out Part C: Line 13 in Part C minus line 6 in Part B			22
Enter the amount from line 18, 19, 20, 21, or (if it applies) 22, **whichever is less**.			23
Enter the amount from line 9 in Part B or the amount from line 14 in Part C, whichever applies to you.		+	24
Line 23 plus line 24. Enter this amount on line 21400 of your return.	**Allowable deduction**	=	25

See the privacy notice on your return.

T778 E (21)   Page 4 of 4

▶可申請費用

✓ 保母

✓ 托兒所

✓ 提供托兒相關服務的教育機構

✓ 日間營地和日間運動學校(以照顧為目的)

✓ 寄宿學校、過夜體育學校或涉及住宿的營地

▶不可申請費用

X 醫療或醫院護理

X 服裝費用

X 交通費用

X 與教育相關的費用，例如常規課程或體育學習課程的學費

X 休閒或娛樂活動的費用，例如網球課或童子軍的學費

▶配偶贍養費

贍養費是夫妻分居或是離婚後，夫妻一方向配偶提供經濟援助所必須支付的金額，一般是按月支付，但也可以一次性支付。在大多數情況下，法院會酌情在離婚/分居時判定一方向另一方支付一筆費用或在分割家庭財產時考慮較為弱勢的一方，此筆配偶贍養費在申報所得稅時可以扣除。

▶撫養扣除額

若您有撫養以下條件之一的被撫養人，則可在申報表上申報扣除：

✓ 您的父母

✓ 您的祖父母

✓ 您未滿18歲的孩子或孫子

✓ 您年滿18歲的孩子或孫子，因身心障礙或無謀生能力需依賴
　您的長期照顧。

▶看護扣除額

如果符合條件的受撫養人年滿18 歲，並且因身心障礙或無謀生能力需依賴您的長期照顧，您可以申請最高 $ 7,348 的看護費用。

如果符合條件的受撫養人未滿18 歲，您可以申請 $ 2,295 的看護費用。

▶收養扣除額

如果您在加拿大合法收養18歲以下兒童，您可以申請與收養之兒童有關的收養費用。每個孩子的最高金額為$ 16,729 。

可申請費用

✓ 支付給收養機構的費用

✓ 收養相關法律及行政費用

✓ 孩子和養父母的合理和必要的旅行和生活費用

✓ 文件翻譯費

✓ 必要的政府規費及各項代辦費用

▶醫療費用扣除額

申請對象

✓ 納稅義務人

✓ 配偶或同居伴侶

✓ 未滿 18 歲的子女

✓ 配偶或同居伴侶的未滿18歲子女

可申請醫療費用

✓ 支付給醫療專業人員的費用

✓ 護理相關設備

✓ 醫療必須交通

✓ 義肢、輔助器具

✓ 視力保健

✓ 氧氣瓶、胰島素

✓ 導盲犬

✓ 骨髓或器官移植

✓ 無障礙空間住宅改造或新建

✓ 復健治療

✓ 手語服務

✓ 聾盲患者專業服務

✓ 搬家費用

✓ 輪椅

✓ 看護培訓

✓ 殘疾人士的長期治療

✓ 藥物

✓ 健康檢查

✓ 假牙

✓ 私人醫療保險

✓ 用於醫療目的的醫用大麻相關產品

✓ 生育相關費用

▶計算方式

1.列舉符合資格的醫療費用

2.計算納稅義務人淨收入的3%或是 $ 2,421兩者間較小值

3.第1項減去第2項就是可申報金額

二、教育扣除額：

▶學雜費扣除額

可申請的學費

✓ 專上學校

✓ 加拿大境內外高等學校

✓ 年滿16歲就讀職業培訓為主的學校

不能申請的學費

X 由雇主支付或報銷的費用X 政府補助費用

X 課外活動X 醫藥費用

X 交通費用X 就學期間食宿

X 證照考試費X 學生會入會費

X 書籍費用

▶申請表格

　　想要申請學費扣除額需要從學校取得的正式收據或表格才能證明您在該年度支付的學費金額，前提是您為每間學校支付的費用必須超過 $ 100。舉例來說，假如您一年中同時就讀兩間學校，並取得兩張表格，那麼每張表格都需要超過 $ 100才能申請學費扣除額，若是只有一張超過$ 100就只有一張表格可以申請。

➡加拿大境內的學費及入學證明，需申報表格T2202。

Canada Revenue Agency
Agence du revenu du Canada

Protected B when completed
Protégé B une fois rempli

For student / Pour étudiant

Tuition and Enrolment Certificate
Certificat pour frais de scolarité et d'inscription

Year
Année   **1**

| Name and address of designated educational institution | 11 School type | 12 Flying school or club |
| Nom et adresse de l'établissement d'enseignement | Catégorie d'école | École ou club de pilotage |

| 14 Student number | 15 Filer Account Number |
| Numéro d'étudiant | Numéro de compte du déclarant |

13 Name of program or course		19	20	21	22	23
Nom du programme ou du cours	Session periods	From YY/MM	To YY/MM	Number of months part-time	Number of months full-time	Eligible tuition fees, part-time and full-time
	Périodes d'études	De AA/MM	À AA/MM	Nombre de mois à temps partiel	Nombre de mois à temps plein	Frais de scolarité admissibles pour études à temps partiel et à temps plein
Student Name / Nom de l'étudiant	1					
	2					
Student address / Adresse de l'étudiant	3					
	4					
	Totals / Totaux	24		25		26

Information for students: See the back of Certificate 1. If you want to transfer all or part of your tuition amount, complete the back of Certificate 2.

Renseignements pour les étudiants : Lisez le verso du certificat 1. Si vous désirez transférer une partie ou la totalité de vos frais de scolarité, remplissez le verso du certificat 2.

| 17 Social insurance number (SIN) |
| Numéro d'assurance sociale (NAS) |

Use the privacy notice on the next page.
Consultez l'avis de confidentialité à la page suivante.

T2202 (21)

Canada

Canada Revenue Agency
Agence du revenu du Canada

Protected B when completed
Protégé B une fois rempli

For student / Pour étudiant

Tuition and Enrolment Certificate
Certificat pour frais de scolarité et d'inscription

Year
Année   **2**

| Name and address of designated educational institution | 11 School type | 12 Flying school or club |
| Nom et adresse de l'établissement d'enseignement | Catégorie d'école | École ou club de pilotage |

| 14 Student number | 15 Filer Account Number |
| Numéro d'étudiant | Numéro de compte du déclarant |

13 Name of program or course		19	20	21	22	23
Nom du programme ou du cours	Session periods	From YY/MM	To YY/MM	Number of months part-time	Number of months full-time	Eligible tuition fees, part-time and full-time
	Périodes d'études	De AA/MM	À AA/MM	Nombre de mois à temps partiel	Nombre de mois à temps plein	Frais de scolarité admissibles pour études à temps partiel et à temps plein
Student Name / Nom de l'étudiant	1					
	2					
Student address / Adresse de l'étudiant	3					
	4					
	Totals / Totaux	24		25		26

Information for students: See the back of Certificate 1. If you want to transfer all or part of your tuition amount, complete the back of Certificate 2.

Renseignements pour les étudiants : Lisez le verso du certificat 1. Si vous désirez transférer une partie ou la totalité de vos frais de scolarité, remplissez le verso du certificat 2.

| 17 Social insurance number (SIN) |
| Numéro d'assurance sociale (NAS) |

See the privacy notice on the next page.
Consultez l'avis de confidentialité à la page suivante.

T2202 (21)

Canada

➡️加拿大境外的學費及入學證明，需申報表格TL11A。

Canada Revenue Agency **Agence du revenu du Canada**	**Tuition and Enrolment Certificate – University Outside Canada**	**Protected B** when completed
		Year: 20____

This certificate is used to certify eligibility for claiming tuition fees of a student attending a university outside Canada.
Administrators of educational institutions outside Canada can refer to **Information sheet RC190**, Information for Educational Institutions Outside Canada, at **canada.ca/forms-publications** for details on completing this certificate.

Part 1 – Educational institution's certification

	A Session periods				B Number of months for part-time	C Number of months for full-time
	From		To			
Name of educational institution	Year	Month	Year	Month		
Address of educational institution						
Name of program or course						
Student's name						
				Total ▶		

I certify that:
- the student was registered as a student at this educational institution in a university course as described above during the periods indicated
- out of the total fees paid for the year, $ _____ is the amount paid for tuition, mandatory ancillary fees that all students have to pay (such as fees for health services or athletics other than student association fees), admission, use of a library or a laboratory, examinations, and for getting a degree
- no part of the above amount was levied for other things such as transportation, parking, books, supplies, special equipment, meals, lodging, or initiation or entrance fees for professional organizations
- the total eligible tuition fees indicated above include the eligible tuition fees paid by scholarship income

_____	_____	_____
Authorized officer's name and title (print)	Authorized officer's signature	Date

Part 2 – Information for Students

- To calculate your available tuition, education, and textbook amount, fill out **federal Schedule 11**, Federal Tuition, Education, and Textbook Amounts and Canada Training Credit. Depending on where you live, you also may need to fill out a provincial or territorial Schedule (S11).
- If you want to transfer unused current year amounts to one designated individual, complete Part 3 of this certificate. If you did not reside in the same province or territory as the designated individual on December 31, special rules may apply.
- For more information, see **Guide P105**, Students and Income Tax, and **Information sheet RC192**, Information for Students – Educational Institutions Outside Canada, at **canada.ca/cra-forms-publications**.
- **Do not** send this certificate with your Income Tax and Benefit Return. Keep the certificate in case we ask to see it.

Part 3 – Student's authorization to transfer tuition, education, and textbook amounts

I designate _____ , my _____ , to claim:
　　　　　　　　 Individual's name 　　　　　　　　　　　　　 Relationship to you

(1) $ _____ on line 32400 of their **Income Tax and Benefit Return**, or on line 36000 of their **federal Schedule 2**, as
　　 Federal tuition amount 　 applicable

(2) $ _____ on line 58600 of their **provincial** or **territorial Form 428**, or on line 59090 of their **provincial** or **territorial**
　　 Provincial or territorial 　 **Schedule (S2)**, as applicable
　　 amount

Note 1: Line (1) above cannot be more than the maximum transferable amount on your **federal Schedule 11**.
Note 2: Line (2) above cannot be more than the maximum transferable amount of your **provincial** or **territorial Schedule (S11)**. If you resided in Quebec, Alberta, Ontario or Saskatchewan on December 31, you are not required to fill out line (2) above.

_____	_____	_____
Student's signature	Social insurance number	Date

See the privacy notice on your return.

TL11A E (21)　　　　　　　　　　　(Ce formulaire est disponible en français.)　　　　　　　Canada

➡ 通勤至美國就學的學費及入學證明，需申報表格TL11C。

I+I Canada Revenue Agence du revenu
Agency du Canada

Tuition Fees Certificate – Educational Institutions Outside Canada for a Deemed Resident of Canada

Year: 20___

This certificate is used to certify eligibility for claiming tuition fees of a student who is deemed to be a resident of Canada under section 250 of the Income Tax Act and was enrolled in an educational institution outside Canada that is a university, college or other designated educational institution providing courses at the post-secondary level.

Administrators of educational institutions outside Canada can refer to **Information sheet RC190**, Information for Educational Institutions Outside Canada, **at canada.ca/forms-publications** for details on completing this certificate.

Part 1 - Educational institution's certification

I certify that:

- _____ was enrolled at this institution
  Student's name

- this student was enrolled for the following period(s):   From | Year Month Day | To | Year Month Day |

- out of the total fees paid for the year, $ _____ is the amount paid for tuition, mandatory ancillary fees that all students have to pay (such as fees for health services or athletics other than student association fees), admission, use of a library or a laboratory, examinations, and for getting a degree or diploma

- none of the above amount was levied for other things such as transportation, parking, books, supplies, special equipment, meals, lodging, or initiation or entrance fees for professional organizations

- the total eligible tuition fees indicated above include the eligible tuition fees paid by scholarship income (where applicable)

_____   _____
Name of university, college, or other educational institution   City/Country

_____   _____   _____
Authorized officer's name and title (print)   Authorized officer's signature   Date

---

Part 2 - Information for Students

- To calculate your available tuition, education, and textbook amount, the tuition amount you can transfer to a designated individual, and any unused amounts you can carry to a future year, fill out **federal Schedule 11**, Federal Tuition, Education, and Textbook Amounts and Canada Training Credit. Depending on where you live, you also may need to fill out a provincial or territorial Schedule (S11).

- For more information, see **Guide P105**, Students and Income Tax, and **Information sheet RC192**, Information for Students – Educational Institutions Outside Canada, at **canada.ca/cra-forms-publications**.

- Do **not** send this certificate with your Income Tax and Benefit Return. Keep the certificate in case we ask to see it.

See the privacy notice on your return.

TL11D E (21)   (Ce formulaire est disponible en français.)   Canada

➡被視為加拿大居民就讀加拿大境外的學費及入學證明，需申報表格TL11D。

I✦I Canada Revenue Agence du reven.		**Protected B** when completed

Tuition Fees Certificate – Educational Institutions Outside Canada for a Deemed Resident of Canada

Year: 20 ___

This certificate is used to certify eligibility for claiming tuition fees of a student who is deemed to be a resident of Canada under section 250 of the Income Tax Act and was enrolled in an educational institution outside Canada that is a university, college or other designated educational institution providing courses at the post-secondary level.

Administrators of educational institutions outside Canada can refer to **Information sheet RC190**, Information for Educational Institutions Outside Canada, at **canada.ca/forms-publications** for details on completing this certificate.

Part 1 - Educational institution's certification

I certify that:

• _____ was enrolled at this institution
           Student's name

• this student was enrolled for the following period(s):   From | Year Month Day | To | Year Month Day |

• out of the total fees paid for the year, $ _____ is the amount paid for tuition, mandatory ancillary fees that all students have to pay (such as fees for health services or athletics other than student association fees), admission, use of a library or a laboratory, examinations, and for getting a degree or diploma

• none of the above amount was levied for other things such as transportation, parking, books, supplies, special equipment, meals, lodging, or initiation or entrance fees for professional organizations

• the total eligible tuition fees indicated above include the eligible tuition fees paid by scholarship income (where applicable)

_____   _____
Name of university, college, or other educational institution   City/Country

_____ _____ _____
Authorized officer's name and title (print)   Authorized officer's signature   Date

Part 2 - Information for Students

• To calculate your available tuition, education, and textbook amount, the tuition amount you can transfer to a designated individual, and any unused amounts you can carry to a future year, fill out **federal Schedule 11**, Federal Tuition, Education, and Textbook Amounts and Canada Training Credit. Depending on where you live, you also may need to fill out a provincial or territorial Schedule (S11).

• For more information, see **Guide P105**, Students and Income Tax, and **Information sheet RC192**, Information for Students – Educational Institutions Outside Canada, at **canada.ca/cra-forms-publications**.

• Do **not** send this certificate with your Income Tax and Benefit Return. Keep the certificate in case we ask to see it.

See the privacy notice on your return.

TL11D E (21)   (Ce formulaire est disponible en français.)   Canadä

▶**學貸利息扣除額**

您可以申請當年度或前面5年因學貸而產生的利息費用扣除，若是您在支付利息的當年度沒有應納稅額，建議不要當年度申報此項扣除額，您可以留做未來5年內有應納稅額時做扣抵。

▶**培訓學費扣除額**

加拿大政府每年提供 $ 250的培訓額度，並且可積累至下一年度，如果您在加拿大參加符合條件的培訓課程，且滿足以下所有條件，則可以申請此筆費用：

✓ 當年度整年居住在加拿大

✓ 年齡26~66歲

✓ 當年度或前一年度還有培訓額度

三、殘疾扣除額

如果您的身體或精神功能受損,並且已支付醫療費用,包含行動、心理狀態、聽力、視力、說話等等功能受損,則可以扣除您當年度支付的費用,以便日常生活得以進行工作或上學需求。

▶**殘疾扣除額**

可申請的費用

✓ 護理服務

✓ 盲人打字機

✓ 就業輔導服務

✓ 閱讀服務

✓ 手語服務

✓ 日常必須設備

不可申請的費用

X 已經透過醫療費用申請的費用

▶**申請表格**

➡申請殘疾扣除額需填報表格T929申請

Canada Revenue Agency / **Agence du revenu du Canada**

Disability Supports Deduction

Use this form to calculate the amount to enter on line 21500 of your tax return.

For more information, see "General information" on the back of this form.

Step 1 – Calculate your net disability supports expenses

Column 1 – Device or service	Column 2 – Amount paid	Column 3 – Amount reimbursed or assistance received (if applicable). See "Amounts you cannot claim" on the back of this form.

Enter the total of all amounts in column 2 .... = $ **1**

Enter the total of all amounts in column 3 .... = $ **2**

Subtract line 2 from line 1. This amount is your **net disability supports expenses** .... = $ **3**

If you need more space, use a separate sheet of paper and attach it to this form.

Step 2 – Calculate your disability supports deduction

Enter your **earned income** .... $ **4**

If you attended a designated educational institution or a secondary school at which you were enrolled in an educational program, fill in lines 5 to 12. Otherwise, enter "0" on line 10 and go to line 11.

Enter your **net income** .... $ **5**

Enter your **earned income** from line 4 .... – $ **6**

Line 5 minus line 6 (if negative, enter "0") .... = $ **7**

Enter the number of weeks in the year that you attended the institution or secondary school **8**

× $375

Line 8 multiplied by $375 .... = $ **9**

Enter the amount from line 7 or line 9, whichever is **less**...................... (maximum $15,000) + $ **10**

Add lines 4 and 10 .... = $ **11**

Enter the amount from line 3 or line 11, whichever is **less** .... $ **12**

Enter the amount from line 12 on **line 21500** of your tax return.

T929 E (21)   (Ce formulaire est disponible en français.)   Page 1 of 2

Canada

▶無障礙空間扣除額

申請資格

✓ 獲得殘疾稅收抵免(DTC)　　✓ 年滿65歲以上

符合條件的房屋

✓ 申請人所擁有之房屋　　✓ 土地面積不超過1/2公頃

✓ 長期居住於該房屋

可申請費用

✓ 建築材料　　✓ 安全裝置

✓ 裝修設備使用費用　　✓ 建築計劃費用

✓ 許可證規費　　✓ 水電工

✓ 木匠　　✓ 建築師

不可申請費用

X 個人勞動力費用　　X 個人使用工具的價值

X 購買房屋費用　　X 例行性維修費用

X 家電產品　　X 監視器

X 園藝造景　　X 貸款利息

X 增值性裝修

四、搬家費用扣除額：

▶因就學而搬家

如果您因為就讀大學、學院或其他教育機構的專上課程而搬家，您可以申請符合條件的搬家費用。但是，您只能從您的收入中扣除這筆費用，例如：獎學金、助學金和研究補助金等等。

申請資格

✓ 新家必須比目前居住地距離新學校更靠近至少40公里

✓ 新家必須是長期居住地

✓ 新學校有收入可以報銷搬家費用

▶因工作而搬家

不論是加拿大境內搬家、海外搬入加拿大、加拿大搬至國外或加拿大以外搬家，只要是因為工作調動或是自僱者另覓營業場所而搬家，都可以申請符合條件的搬家費用。

申請資格

✓ 不論是加拿大境內搬家、海外搬入加拿大、加拿大搬至國外或加拿大以外搬家，新家必須比目前居住地距離新工作地點更靠近至少40公里。

✓ 新家必須是長期居住地

✓ 新工作有收入可以報銷搬家費用

可申請搬家費用

✓ 搬家貨運費用

✓ 移動至新家交通費、餐費及住宿費

✓ 臨時居住最多15天餐費及住宿費

✓ 提前解約房租費用

✓ 更換駕照費用

✓ 舊屋空置稅金、水電等等費用(最高 $ 5000)

✓ 出售舊屋費用

不可申請費用

X 出售舊屋損失

X 出售舊屋廣告

X 新屋未確定前旅行費用

X 新工作未確定前旅行費用

X 留置舊屋的物品價值

X 舊屋為恢復原狀之清潔整修費用

X 郵資

X 未積極出售舊屋所產生之舊屋空置費用

▶申請表格

➡申請搬家費用需填報T1-M表格申請

Canada Revenue Agency   Agence du revenu du Canada

Protected B when completed

Moving Expenses Deduction

Before completing this form, read "Information About Moving Expenses" included with this form.

Complete a separate form for each move to calculate your eligible moving expenses deductions.

If you are filing electronically or filing a paper return, do not send any documents. Keep all of your supporting documents in case you are asked to provide them later. If you are using EFILE, show your documents to your EFILE service provider.

Tax year ▶

Part 1 – Taxpayer information

First name	Last name	Social insurance number

Part 2 – Calculation of distance in kilometres

Distance in kilometres between your **old** home and your **new** place of work or educational institution		1
Distance in kilometres between your **new** home and your **new** place of work or educational institution	−	2
Line 1 minus line 2	=	3

If the amount on line 3 is **less than** 40 kilometres, you **cannot** deduct your moving expenses.
If this is the case, do **not** complete the rest of this form.

Part 3 – Details of the move

	Year	Month	Day
Date of move			

	Year	Month	Day
Date you started to work, run a business or study full time at a new location			

Main reason for the move   ☐ To work or to run a business   **or**   ☐ To study full time

Address of your old home

Apt No. – Street No. Street name		
City	Province or territory	Postal or ZIP code
Country (if outside Canada)		

Address of your new home

Apt No. – Street No. Street name		
City	Province or territory	Postal or ZIP code
Country (if outside Canada)		

Information about your employer, business, or educational institution after the move

Name		
Apt No. – Street No. Street name		
City	Province or territory	Postal or ZIP code
Country (if outside Canada)		

T1-M E (21)   (Ce formulaire est disponible en français.)   Page 4 of 6   **Canadä**

五、居家辦公費用扣除額：

由於COVID-19大流行，2020~2022年間越來越多企業規劃員工居家辦公，但是居家辦公會產生一些額外的費用，例如：辦公用品、電話費、電費等等，申請方式分為兩種：

▶簡易申報

雇主無須填寫並簽署表格，申請人無須保留證明文件，也不須確定各項費用金額。

申請資格

因COVID-19在一年中(2020~2022年)連續四周超過50%的時間在家工作之居家辦公員工

✓ 雇主沒有補助居家辦公費用

申請費用

✓ 居家工作每天可申請 $ 2

✓ 每年可申請最多 $ 500 (2020年最多 $ 400)

▶詳細申報

雇主須填寫並簽署表格

申請資格

✓ 因COVID-19在一年中(2020~2022年)連續四周超過50%的
　時間在家工作之居家辦公員工

✓ 雇主要求居家辦公

✓ 雇主沒有補助居家辦公費用

申請費用

✓ 依費用證明文件實支實付

✓ 需有雇主填寫並簽署T2200S 表格/T2200 表格

可申請費用

✓ 電費　　　　　　　✓ 冷氣費

✓ 水費　　　　　　　✓ 公寓的公共費用

✓ 網路費　　　　　　✓ 維修費

✓ 租金　　　　　　　✓ 家庭保險

✓ 工作需要之電腦、印表機等等

不可申請費用

X 房屋貸款利息　　　　　X 家具費用

X 資本支出(例：更換家電)　X 裝修費用

▶申請表格

➡因COVID-19而在家工作的就業條件聲明，由雇主填寫並簽署T2200S表格。

Canada Revenue Agency / Agence du revenu du Canada

Protected B when completed

Declaration of Conditions of Employment for Working at Home Due to COVID-19

This form is only for employees who worked from their home in 2021 due to COVID-19. The **employer** must complete and sign this form if the employee chooses to use the detailed method to calculate their home office expenses (work-space-in-the-home and supplies). If the employee is required to pay for expenses other than home office expenses, do not use this form. Instead, complete Form T2200, Declaration of Conditions of Employment.

The **employee** does **not** need to attach this form to their return, but they must keep it in case we ask to see it later. However, the employee must complete Form T777S, Statement of Employment Expenses for Working at Home Due to COVID-19, and attach it to their tax return to deduct home office expenses for the year.

For more information about claiming employment expenses, see Guide T4044, Employment Expenses.

Part A – Employee information

Last name	First name	Tax year 2021
Employer address		

Part B – Conditions of employment

1. Did this employee work from home due to COVID-19? ☐ Yes ☐ No

2. Did you or will you reimburse this employee for any of their home office expenses? ☐ Yes ☐ No

3. Was the amount included on this employee's T4 slip? ☐ Yes ☐ No

Employer declaration

I certify that this employee worked from home in 2021 due to COVID-19, and was required to pay some or all their own home office expenses used directly in their work while carrying out their duties of employment during that period.

I certify that the information given on this form is, to the best of my knowledge, correct and complete.

Note: Clearly print the name and telephone number of the authorized person in case we need to call to verify information.

Name of employer	Name and title of authorized person
	ext.
Date	Telephone number	Signature of employer or authorized person

The employee has to complete this section if we ask them to send us this form.

Name of employee	Social insurance number	Date
Home address		

See the privacy notice on your return.

T2200S E (21)   (Ce formulaire est disponible en français.)

Canada

➡因工作需求而在家工作的就業條件聲明，由雇主填寫並簽署 T2200表格。

| Canada Revenue Agency / Agence du revenu du Canada | | **Protected B** when completed |

Declaration of Conditions of Employment

The **employer** must complete this form for the employee to deduct employment expenses from their income.

The **employee** does not have to file this form with their return, but must keep it in case we ask to see it. For details about claiming employment expenses, see Guide T4044, Employment Expenses, or the following archived interpretation bulletins: IT352R2 – Employee's Expenses, Including Work Space in Home Expenses, and IT522R – Vehicle, Travel and Sales Expenses of Employees.

Part A – Employee information (please print)

Last name	First name	Tax year
Employer address		
Job title and brief description of duties		

Part B – Conditions of employment

1. Did this employee's contract require them to pay their own expenses while carrying out the duties of employment? ☐ Yes ☐ No

   Answer **yes** even if you provide an allowance or a reimbursement in respect of some or all such expenses.

   If **no**, the employee is **not** entitled to claim employment expenses, and **you are not required to answer any of the other questions.**

2. Did you normally require this employee to travel to locations that were not your place of business or between different locations of your places of business, during the course of performing their employment duties? ☐ Yes ☐ No

   If **yes**, what was the employee's area of travel (be specific)? _____

3. Did you require this employee to be away for at least 12 **consecutive** hours from the municipality and metropolitan area (if there is one) of your business where the employee normally reported for work? ☐ Yes ☐ No

   If **yes**, how frequently? _____

4. Indicate the period(s) of employment during the year: From [Year | Month | Day] to [Year | Month | Day]

   If there was a break in employment, specify dates: _____

5. Did this employee receive or were they entitled to receive a motor vehicle allowance? ☐ Yes ☐ No

   If **yes**, indicate:

   • the amount received as a fixed allowance, such as a flat monthly allowance $_____

   • the per km rate used _____ ($/km), and the amount received $_____

   • the amount of the allowance that was included on the employee's T4 slip $_____

   Did this employee have the use of a company vehicle? ☐ Yes ☐ No

   Was the employee responsible for any of the expenses incurred for the company vehicle? ☐ Yes ☐ No

   If **yes**, indicate the amount and type of expenses:

Amount	Type of expense
$_____	_____
$_____	_____
$_____	_____

六、養老金和儲蓄計劃扣除額：

若是您在應課稅年度有養老金金額調整、註冊退休金計劃(RPP)、註冊退休儲蓄計劃(RRSP)、分割養老金等等退休金計劃或儲蓄相關費用，則可以申請此項所得稅扣除額。

申請表格

➡️ 加拿大養老金計劃存款扣除需填寫表格CPT20申報

Canada Revenue Agency / Agence du revenu du Canada

Protected B when completed

Election To Pay Canada Pension Plan Contributions

You can elect to pay Canada Pension Plan (CPP) contributions if **one** of the following applies:
- You were a resident of Canada for income tax purposes during the year receiving income from any of the types of employment listed on the next page
- You were an individual registered or entitled to be registered under the Indian Act receiving tax-exempt self-employment earnings on a reserve in Canada

To calculate your additional CPP contributions, complete and attach to your return a copy of Schedule 8, Canada Pension Plan Contributions and Overpayments for 2021, or Form RC381, Inter-provincial Calculation for CPP and QPP Contributions and Overpayments for 2021, whichever applies.

You have to file your election **on or before June 15, 2023,** and pay your required contributions **on or before April 30, 2023.**
Complete and attach this form to your return, or send it to the Canada Revenue Agency separately.

Election for the year ▶ **2021**

First name	Last name	Social insurance number (SIN)
Mailing address		
City	Province or territory	Postal code

Part A – Earnings that you elect to pay additional CPP contributions on

Total of your employment earnings as shown on T4 slips (from Part B)		1
Total of your other employment earnings (from Part B)	2	
Tax-exempt self-employment earnings as an individual registered or entitled to be registered under the Indian Act on a reserve (complete Part C)	+ 3	
Line 2 plus line 3	= ▶ +	4
Line 1 plus line 4	(maximum $61,600) =	5
Enter **whichever is less:** amount from line 1 above, or amount from line 4 of Part 3 of your Schedule 8 or amount from line 13 of Part 3 of your Form RC381, whichever applies.	–	6
Line 5 minus line 6 (if negative, enter "0")	–	7
Total of your CPP contributions deducted (from Part B)	÷ 0.0545 = –	8
Line 7 minus line 8	=	9
Total of your Quebec Pension Plan contributions deducted (from Part B)	÷ 0.0590 =	10
Earnings that you can elect to pay additional CPP contributions on: Line 9 minus line 10 (if negative, enter "0")	=	11
Enter **whichever is less:** amount from line 4 or line 11.	12	
Employment earnings not shown on a T4 slip that you elect to pay additional CPP **contributions on:** Enter an amount that is not more than the amount from line 12. Enter this amount on **line 50373** of your Schedule 8 or **line 50373** in Part 4 of your Form RC381, whichever applies.	–	13
Line 11 minus line 13 If you are electing to pay additional CPP contributions on employment earnings shown on your T4 slips, enter this amount on **line 50399** in Part 5 of your Schedule 8 or **line 50399** in Part 4 of your Form RC381, whichever applies.	=	14

CPT20 E (21)   (Ce formulaire est disponible en français.)   Page 1 of 3   **Canadä**

➡️加拿大退休儲蓄計劃存款扣除需填寫表格5000-S8申報

T1-2021　　　　　　　　　　　Protected B when completed

Canada Pension Plan
Contributions and Overpayment
Schedule 8

The Canada Pension Plan (CPP) was amended to provide for the enhancement of pensions. The government of Quebec also adopted legislative amendments to enhance the Quebec Pension Plan (QPP) in a similar way as the federal plan. The enhancements are funded by additional enhanced contributions that began in January 2019.

The contributions consist of a base amount and an enhanced amount. As an employee, your employer will have already deducted the contributions from your salary and wages. As a self-employed individual, you will calculate your required contributions (if any) on this schedule including the base and the enhanced amounts.

For more information, see lines 22200, 22215, 30800, and 31000 of the Federal Income Tax and Benefit Guide.

Is this form for you?

Complete this schedule to calculate your required CPP contributions or overpayment for 2021 if you were a resident of a province or territory **other than Quebec** on December 31, 2021, and you have **no** earned income from the province of Quebec. **Attach** a copy of this schedule to your paper return.

Do **not** complete this schedule if **any** of your T4 slips show QPP contributions. **Instead**, complete Form RC381, Inter-provincial Calculation for CPP and QPP Contributions and Overpayments.

Which parts of this schedule do you need to complete?

Part 1 – Complete this part if you are electing to **stop** contributing to the CPP or you are **revoking** a prior election.

Part 2 – Complete this part to determine the number of months for the CPP contributions calculation.

Part 3 – Complete this part if you are reporting employment income.

Part 4 – Complete this part if you are reporting **only** self-employment income or other earnings you are electing to pay CPP contributions on.

Part 5 – Complete this part if you are reporting employment income **and** self-employment income or other earnings you are electing to pay CPP contributions on. (You must first complete Part 3.)

Part 1 – Election to stop contributing to the CPP or revocation of a prior election

You were considered a CPP working beneficiary and were required to make CPP contributions in 2021 if you met **all** of the following conditions:

- You were 60 to 70 years of age
- You received a CPP or QPP retirement pension
- You had employment and/or self-employment income

However, if you were **at least 65 years of age but under 70 years of age**, you can elect to stop paying CPP contributions.

Employment income

If you had employment income for 2021 and you elected in 2021 to stop paying CPP contributions or revoked in 2021 an election made in a previous year, you should have already completed and sent Form CPT30, Election to Stop Contributing to the Canada Pension Plan or Revocation of a Prior Election, to the Canada Revenue Agency (CRA) and your employer(s).

Self-employment income only

If you had **only** self-employment income for 2021 and are electing in 2021 to **stop** paying CPP contributions on your self-employment earnings, enter the month in 2021 you are choosing to start this election on line 50372 on the next page. The date **cannot** be earlier than the month you turn 65 years of age and are receiving a CPP or QPP retirement pension. For example, if you turn 65 in June, you can choose any month from June to December. If you choose the month of June, enter "06" on line 50372.

If, in 2021, you are **revoking** an election made in a previous year on contributions on self-employment earnings, enter the month in 2021 you are choosing to revoke this election on line 50374 on the next page. Your election remains valid until you revoke it or turn 70 years of age. If you start receiving employment income (other than employment income earned in Quebec) in a future year, you will need to complete Form CPT30 in that year for your election to remain valid.

➡ 美國退休計劃的員工存款屬於臨時分配者需填寫表格RC267申報

Canada Revenue Agency / Agence du revenu du Canada

Protected B when completed
2021

Employee Contributions to a United States Retirement Plan – Temporary Assignments

Complete this form if you are temporarily working in Canada and you continue to participate in a qualifying retirement plan offered by your employer in the United States (U.S.).

You may be able to claim a deduction for the contributions you made to the U.S. plan on your Canadian income tax and benefit return. A 401(k) arrangement is among the qualifying U.S. retirement plans. For a complete list of qualifying U.S. retirement plans, go to **canada.ca/cra-annex-b-convention-canada-usa** (paragraph 10(b)).

Notes
If you are a Canadian resident who commutes or otherwise travels to the U.S. to perform employment services, and you are a member of a qualifying retirement plan of your employer in the U.S., see Form RC268, Employee Contributions to a United States Retirement Plan – Cross-Border Commuters.

If you contributed to an employer-sponsored pension plan or to a social security arrangement in a country other than the U.S., see Form RC269, Employee Contributions to a Foreign Pension Plan or Social Security Arrangement – Non-United States Plans or Arrangements.

You can deduct your contributions to your U.S. retirement plan on your Canadian income tax and benefit return if **all** of the following conditions are met:

- the remuneration you received for the services you performed as an employee in Canada is taxable in Canada
- just before you began performing services in Canada, you were participating in the U.S. plan and you were not a resident of Canada
- the contributions are attributable to employment services you performed in Canada and were made during the period you performed the services
- you are not accruing benefits in, or contributing to, a registered pension plan, deferred profit-sharing plan, registered retirement savings plan (RRSP), specified pension plan, or pooled registered pension plan in Canada for the period you performed the services
- you have not performed services in Canada for the same employer (or a related employer) for more than 60 of the 120 months preceding 2021

Do not attach any statements of your contributions to your paper return, but keep them in case the Canada Revenue Agency (CRA) asks to see them.

Report all amounts in Canadian dollars. For information about exchange rates, see "Report foreign income and other foreign amounts" in Step 2 of the Income Tax and Benefit Guide for Non-Residents and Deemed Residents of Canada.

Calculating your deduction

Amount of your 2021 contributions to the U.S. retirement plan		1
Amount of contributions that would qualify for tax relief in the U.S. if you were a resident of the U.S. and performed your services in the U.S.		2
Enter **whichever is less:** amount from line 1 or line 2. Add this amount to the amount on **line 20700** of your return.	51204	3

Pension adjustment

If you receive a T4 slip, your employer will have to calculate and report a pension adjustment (PA) to the CRA. Enter on line 20600 of your return the total of all amounts shown in box 52 of your T4 slips. The PA will reduce your RRSP contribution room for 2022.

If you do not receive a T4 slip showing your PA, calculate and report it as follows:

Your **resident compensation** of 2021 (1)	51220		4
Rate	×	18%	5
Line 4 multiplied by the percentage on line 5	=	▶	6
Money purchase limit of 2021		29,210 00	7
Enter **whichever is less:** amount from line 6 or line 7. Add this amount to the amount on **line 20600** of your return.	51230		8

(1) Your **resident compensation** for 2021 is the total of your salaries, wages, and other amounts from your employment with the employer in question, excluding amounts that are exempt from income tax in Canada according to the Canada-U.S. tax convention.

See the privacy notice on your return.

➡️ 美國退休計劃的員工存款屬於跨境通勤者需填寫表格RC268申報

Employee Contributions to a United States Retirement Plan – Cross-Border Commuters

Complete this form if you are a Canadian resident who commutes or otherwise travels to the United States (U.S.) to perform employment services, and you are a member of a qualifying retirement plan of your employer in the U.S. A 401(k) arrangement is among the qualifying U.S. retirement plans. For a complete list of qualifying U.S. retirement plans, go to **canada.ca/cra-annex-b-convention-canada-usa** (paragraph 10(b)).

Note
If you are temporarily working in Canada and you continue to participate in a qualifying retirement plan offered by your employer in the U.S., see Form RC267, Employee Contributions to a United States Retirement Plan – Temporary Assignments.

You can deduct your contributions to your U.S. retirement plan on your Canadian income tax and benefit return if **all** of the following conditions are met:

- the remuneration you received for the services you performed as an employee in the U.S. is taxable in the U.S.
- your employer is a resident of the U.S. or has a permanent establishment in the U.S.
- the contributions are attributable to the services you performed as an employee in the U.S., for which you received U.S. taxable remuneration, and are made during the period you performed those services

The amount you can deduct can be no more than the amount of tax relief available in the U.S., and no more than your registered retirement savings plan (RRSP) deduction room remaining after you deduct any RRSP contributions for the year.

Do not attach any statements of your contributions to your paper return, but keep them in case the Canada Revenue Agency ask to see them.

Report all amounts in Canadian dollars. For information about exchange rates, see "Report foreign income and other foreign amounts" in Step 2 of the Income Tax and Benefit Guide for Non-Residents and Deemed Residents of Canada.

Calculating your deduction

Amount of your 2021 contributions to the U.S. retirement plan		1
Amount of contributions that would qualify for tax relief in the U.S. if you were a resident of the U.S. and performed your services in the U.S.		2
Enter **whichever is less:** amount from line 1 or line 2.	51205	3
2021 RRSP deduction limit		4
Amount from line 16 of Schedule 7	−	5
Line 4 minus line 5	=	6
Enter **whichever is less:** amount from line 3 or line 6. Add this amount to the amount on **line 20700** of your return.		7

→美國以外其他外國退休養老金計劃的員工存款需填寫表格 RC269申報

<table>
<tr><td>**I✦I** Canada Revenue Agency   Agence du revenu du Canada</td><td>**Protected B** when completed
2021</td></tr>
</table>

Employee Contributions to a Foreign Pension Plan or Social Security Arrangement – Non-United States Plans or Arrangements

Complete Part A of this form if you contributed in 2021 to a **social security arrangement** in **any** of the following countries:

Chile	Finland	Germany	Ireland	Lithuania	Slovenia	Switzerland
Estonia	France	Greece	Latvia	Netherlands	Sweden	

Complete Part B of this form if you contributed in 2021 to an **employer-sponsored pension plan** in **any** of the following countries:

Chile	Estonia	Germany	Italy	Netherlands	Sweden	Venezuela
Colombia	Finland	Greece	Latvia	Slovenia	Switzerland	
Ecuador	France	Ireland	Lithuania	South Africa	United Kingdom	

The **Canadian Competent Authority** has to agree that foreign social security arrangements generally correspond to the Canada Pension Plan (CPP) and that foreign pension plans generally correspond to a Canadian registered pension plan (RPP).

For more information on **eligible** foreign social security arrangements and **eligible** foreign employer-sponsored pension plans, go to **canada.ca/cra-guidance-tax-treaty-relief-cross-border-pension-contributions**.

For information on how to contact the Canadian Competent Authority (Legislative Policy Directorate), go to **canada.ca/cra-competent-authority-services**.

If you participated in your employer's retirement plan in the United States, see Form RC267, Employee Contributions to a United States Retirement Plan – Temporary Assignments, and Form RC268, Employee Contributions to a United States Retirement Plan – Cross-Border Commuters.

A statement from your employer or the plan administrator will indicate the amount of your contributions. Do not send us this statement, but keep it in case Canada Revenue Agency (CRA) ask to see it.

Report all amounts in Canadian dollars. For information about exchange rates, see "Report foreign income and other foreign amounts" in Step 2 of the Income Tax and Benefit Guide for Non-Residents and Deemed Residents of Canada.

七、非居民納稅義務人扣除額限制：

　　一般來說，加拿大非居民納稅人及稅務居民在申報所得稅時，所適用的扣除項目是相同的，除了以下兩點有條件限制：

▶托兒費用

　　只有非居民納稅義務人向稅務居民支付的托兒費用且地點在加拿大才可以申請。

▶搬家費用

　　加拿大非居民納稅義務人通常無法申請扣除搬家費用，若是全日制學生有獎學金、助學金等等所得申報，則可以申請搬家費用扣除。

肆、個人免稅額：

　　加拿大跟台灣的稅制一樣會有許多可以列舉扣除的項目，納稅人須根據自身的具體情況，和各稅收抵免項目的適用範圍來確定可適用的稅收抵免項目和扣除額，將已支出費用從收入中扣除，例如：撫養扣除額、教育扣除額等等，可以讓納稅義務人在納稅申報表上申報的扣除、抵免和費用，以幫助減少您必須支付的稅額。以下詳細介紹加拿大各種稅前扣除額：

一、基本個人免稅額(BPA)：

基本個人免稅額是一項不可退稅（non-refundable）的稅收抵免，替在加拿大生活或工作的個人提供聯邦所得稅減免。所謂的不可退稅，指的是如果你的稅收抵免總額高於所得稅額，差額不予退還。

▶申請資格

收入低於BPA → 全額減免

收入高於BPA → 部分減免

▶加拿大BPA

淨收入大於$214,368 → BPA=$12,298

淨收入小於$150,473 → 2020年BPA=$13,229

2021年BPA=$13,808

2022年BPA=$14,398

2023年BPA=$15,000

按照15%的聯邦稅率計算，加拿大納稅人2022年的BPA稅收抵免最高可達14398*0.15=$2,160。

二、兒童福利(CCB)：

▶申請資格

須滿足以下所有條件：

1.您與未滿18歲的孩子同住

2.您是主要照顧者

3.您是加拿大稅務居民

4.您或是配偶屬於加拿大公民、永久居民及住滿18個月且持續持有居住許可的臨時居民其中之一。

▶申請金額

金額依照居住省分、孩童年紀、申報人所得不同而有不同的金額。

▶申請表格

➡申請兒童福利免稅額，需填寫表格RC66。

| | Canada Revenue Agency | Agence du revenu du Canada | | **Protected B** when completed |

Canada Child Benefits Application
includes federal, provincial, and territorial programs

Find out if this form is for you
Fill out this form to apply for the Canada child benefit and register your children for the goods and services tax/harmonized sales tax (GST/HST) credit, the climate action incentive payment (CAIP) and related federal, provincial, or territorial programs the Canada Revenue Agency (CRA) administers. You can also use this form if you started a shared-custody situation for one or more children.

Do not fill out this form if you already applied using My Account on the CRA website or when you registered the birth of your newborn with your province or territory (except Yukon and Nunavut).

Who should fill out this form
The person who is **primarily responsible** for the care and upbringing of the child should apply (see "Primarily responsible for the care and upbringing of the child" on page 3).

When a child resides with a female parent in the home, the female parent is usually considered to be primarily responsible for the child and should apply. However, if the child's other parent is primarily responsible, they should apply and attach a signed letter from the female parent stating that the other parent with whom she resides is primarily responsible for all the children in the home. If the child lives with same-sex parents, only one parent should apply for all the children in the home.

For more information
For more information on the Canada child benefit, including eligibility requirements, go to **canada.ca/cra-benefits**, see Booklet T4114, Canada Child Benefit, or call **1-800-387-1193**. From outside Canada or the United States, call **1-613-940-8495**. We accept collect calls by automated response.

Step 1 – Your information
Social insurance number (SIN):

If you do not have a SIN, see Booklet T4114, Canada Child Benefit, under "How to apply."

First name:

Last name:

Date of birth: __ Year Month Day

Your language of correspondence: ☐ English ☐ Français

Phone numbers: Home: _____ Work: _____ Ext: _____ Cell: _____

Step 2 – Your address
Mailing address

Apt. No. – Street No., Street name, PO Box, RR:

City:

Province or territory (or country if outside Canada):

Postal or ZIP code:

Have you moved from a different province or territory within the last 12 months? ☐ Yes ☐ No

If **yes**, enter the previous province or territory and the date you moved: _____ Date: __ Year Month Day

Home address ☐ Same as mailing address

Apt. No. – Street No., Street name, RR:

City:

Province or territory (or country if outside Canada):

Postal or ZIP code:

Canada

三、殘疾稅收抵免 (DTC)：

DTC 可以減少有身體或精神障礙的人或其照顧者可能須支付的所得稅金額，目的在於抵銷付出的費用或成本。

▶申請資格

如果醫生證明您在以下類別中一項嚴重及長期的功能喪失，或是二項類別對生活造成嚴重不便或是需要接受治療才能維持功能。

■行走：花費時間是同齡人的3倍，且持續一年以上以及每日90%以上時間。

■聽力：在安靜的環境中聽懂口語對話所花費時間是同齡人的3倍，且持續一年以上以及每日90%以上時間。

■心理：有嚴重且長期的障礙，限制了執行日常生活所需的心理功能的能力，例如適應能力、專注力、判斷力、記憶力、情緒調節能力等等。

■說話：在安靜的情況下表達說話讓人理解所花費時間是同齡人的3倍，且持續一年以上以及每日90%以上時間。

■穿衣：自己穿衣服所花費時間是同齡人的3倍，且持續一年以上以及每日90%以上時間。

■視力：經過矯正後雙眼視力在20/200以下或是視野在20度以下，且持續一年以上以及每日90%以上時間。

■進食：自己準備食物或進食所花費時間是同齡人的3倍，且持續一年以上以及每日90%以上時間。

■維生:需要依靠以下治療維生洗腎、胰島素注射、氧氣、插管等等,每周至少2次,每周至少14小時,且持續達一年以上。

■排泄:排泄所花費時間是同齡人的3倍,且持續一年以上以及每日90%以上時間。

▶申請表格

➡申請殘疾稅收抵免,需填寫表格T2201。

Canada Revenue Agency Agence du revenu du Canada

Protected B
when completed

Disability Tax Credit Certificate

Help
canada.ca/disability
-tax-credit
1-800-959-8281

The information provided in this form will be used by the Canada Revenue Agency (CRA) to determine the eligibility of the individual applying for the disability tax credit (DTC). For more information, see the general information on page 16.

Part A – Individual's section

1) Tell us about **the person with the disability**

First name:

Last name:

Social insurance number:

Mailing address:

City:

Province or territory:

Postal code:

Date of birth: Year Month Day

2) Tell us about **the person claiming the disability amount**

☐ The person with the disability is claiming the disability amount

(or)

☐ A supporting family member is claiming the disability amount (the spouse or common-law partner of the person with the disability, or a parent, grandparent, child, grandchild, brother, sister, uncle, aunt, nephew, or niece of that person or their spouse or common-law partner).

First name:

Last name:

Relationship:

Social insurance number: Does the person with the disability live with you? ☐ Yes ☐ No

Indicate which of the basic necessities of life have been regularly and consistently provided to the person with the disability, and the years for which it was provided:

☐ Food _____ Year(s) ☐ Shelter _____ Year(s) ☐ Clothing _____ Year(s)

Provide details regarding the support you provide to the person with the disability (regularity of the support, proof of dependency, if the person lives with you, etc.):

If you want to provide more information than the space allows, use a separate sheet of paper, sign it, and attach it to this form. Make sure to include the name of the person with the disability.

As the supporting family member claiming the disability amount, I confirm that the information provided is accurate.

Signature:

T2201 E (22) (Ce formulaire est disponible en français.) Page 1 of 16

Canada

四、兒童殘疾津貼(CDB)：

▶申請資格

1. 申請人必須有資格獲得加拿大兒童福利 (CCB)

2. 8歲以下孩童必須有資格獲得殘疾稅收抵免(DTC)

▶可申請額度計算

依照符合條件的兒童人數、家庭淨收入、婚姻狀況來核定，詳如下表：

調整後的家庭淨收入（$）	一名符合條件的受撫養人（$/月）	兩名符合條件的受撫養人（$/月）	三名符合條件的受撫養人（$/月）
未達 $71,060	$248.75	$497.50	$746.25
$75,000	$238.24	$478.79	$727.54
$80,000	$224.91	$455.04	$703.79
$85,000	$211.58	$431.29	$680.04
$95,000	$184.91	$383.79	$632.54
$105,000	$158.24	$336.29	$585.04
$115,000	$131.58	$288.79	$537.54
$125,000	$104.91	$241.29	$490.04

調整後的家庭 淨收入（$）	一名符合條件 的受撫養人 （$/月）	兩名符合條件 的受撫養人 （$/月）	三名符合條件 的受撫養人 （$/月）
$135,000	$78.24	$193.79	$442.54
$145,000	$51.58	$146.29	$395.04
$155,000	$24.91	$98.79	$347.54
$165,000	$0.00	$51.29	$300.04
$175,000	$0.00	$3.79	$252.54
$185,000	$0.00	$0.00	$205.04
$195,000	$0.00	$0.00	$157.54
$205,000	$0.00	$0.00	$110.04
$215,000	$0.00	$0.00	$62.54
$225,000	$0.00	$0.00	$15.04
$235,000	$0.00	$0.00	$0.00

五、家庭無障礙稅收抵免：

▶申請資格

1.年滿65歲以上

2.必須有資格獲得殘疾稅收抵免(DTC)

▶可申請的費用

✓ 建築材料	✓ 固定裝置
✓ 設備租賃	✓ 建築計劃
✓ 許可費用	✓ 水電工
✓ 木匠	✓ 建築師

▶不可申請的費用

X 購買房產	X 例行性維修
X 購買家電	X 購買家用娛樂產品
X 維護費用	X 貸款費用

六、GST/HST抵免：

商品和服務稅/統一銷售稅 (GST/HST) 抵免可幫助中低收入的個人和家庭抵免他們支付的 GST 或 HST。

▶申請資格

通常中低收入的加拿大稅務居民，都可以申請GST/HST抵免。

▶可申請額度計算

依照受撫養兒童人數、家庭淨收入、婚姻狀況來核定，詳如下表：

單身淨收入($)	沒有小孩 ($/年)	1個小孩 ($/年)	2個小孩 ($/年)	3個小孩 ($/年)	4個小孩 ($/年)
未達 $9,919	$306	$773	$934	$1,095	$1,256
$12,000	$347.62	$773	$934	$1,095	$1,256
$15,000	$407.62	$773	$934	$1,095	$1,256
$20,000	$467	$773	$934	$1,095	$1,256
$25,000	$467	$773	$934	$1,095	$1,256
$30,000	$467	$773	$934	$1,095	$1,256
$35,000	$467	$773	$934	$1,095	$1,256
$40,000	$458.3	$764.3	$925.3	$1,086.3	$1,247.3
$45,000	$208.3	$514.3	$675.3	$836.3	$997.3
$50,000	$0	$264.3	$425.3	$586.3	$747.3
$55,000	$0	$14.3	$175.3	$336.3	$497.3
$60,000	$0	$0	$0	$86.3	$247.3
$65,000	$0	$0	$0	$0	$0

家庭淨 收入($)	沒有小孩 ($/年)	1個小孩 ($/年)	2個小孩 ($/年)	3個小孩 ($/年)	4個小孩 ($/年)
未達 $39,826	$612	$773	$934	$1,095	$1,256
$40,000	$603.3	$764.3	$925.3	$1,086.3	$1,247.3
$45,000	$353.3	$514.3	$675.3	$836.3	$997.3
$50,000	$103.3	$264.3	$425.3	$586.3	$747.3
$55,000	$0	$14.3	$175.3	$336.3	$497.3
$60,000	$0	$0	$0	$86.3	$247.3
$65,000	$0	$0	$0	$0	$0

▶申請表格

➡如果有孩子，填寫RC66表格。

Canada Revenue Agency — Agence du revenu du Canada

Canada Child Benefits Application
includes federal, provincial, and territorial programs

Find out if this form is for you

Fill out this form to apply for the Canada child benefit and register your children for the goods and services tax/harmonized sales tax (GST/HST) credit, the climate action incentive payment (CAIP) and related federal, provincial, or territorial programs the Canada Revenue Agency (CRA) administers. You can also use this form if you started a shared-custody situation for one or more children.

Do not fill out this form if you already applied using My Account on the CRA website or when you registered the birth of your newborn with your province or territory (except Yukon and Nunavut).

Who should fill out this form

The person who is **primarily responsible** for the care and upbringing of the child should apply (see "Primarily responsible for the care and upbringing of the child" on page 3).

When a child resides with a female parent in the home, the female parent is usually considered to be primarily responsible for the child and should apply. However, if the child's other parent is primarily responsible, they should apply and attach a signed letter from the female parent stating that the other parent with whom she resides is primarily responsible for all the children in the home. If the child lives with same-sex parents, only one parent should apply for all the children in the home.

For more information

For more information on the Canada child benefit, including eligibility requirements, go to **canada.ca/cra-benefits**, see Booklet T4114, Canada Child Benefit, or call **1-800-387-1193**. From outside Canada or the United States, call **1-613-940-8495**. We accept collect calls by automated response.

Step 1 – Your information

Social insurance number (SIN):

If you do not have a SIN, see Booklet T4114, Canada Child Benefit, under "How to apply."

First name:

Last name:

Date of birth: _____ Year   Month   Day

Your language of correspondence: ☐ English   ☐ Français

Phone numbers: Home: _____   Work: _____   Ext: _____   Cell: _____

Step 2 – Your address

Mailing address

Apt. No. – Street No., Street name, PO Box, RR:

City:

Province or territory (or country if outside Canada):

Postal or ZIP code:

Have you moved from a different province or territory within the last 12 months? ☐ Yes   ☐ No

If **yes**, enter the previous province or territory and the date you moved: _____   Date: _____ Year   Month   Day

Home address   ☐ Same as mailing address

Apt. No. – Street No., Street name, RR:

City:

Province or territory (or country if outside Canada):

Postal or ZIP code:

Canada

➡如果沒有孩子，填寫RC151表格。

Canada Revenue Agency | Agence du revenu du Canada

Protected B when completed

GST/HST Credit and Climate Action Incentive Payment Application for Individuals Who Become Residents of Canada

Fill out this form to apply for the GST/HST credit, including related provincial and territorial programs, and the climate action incentive payment, for the year in which you became a resident of Canada. Use this form **only** if you don't have children. If you have children under 19 years of age, use My Account or Form RC66, Canada Child Benefits Application.

For more information, see "General information" on pages 3 and 4.

Step 1 – Your information

First name | Last name | Social Insurance number

Date of birth: Year | Month | Day | Home telephone number | Work telephone number

Mailing address (Apt No – Street No Street name, PO Box, RR)

Your language of correspondence: ☐ English

City | Province or territory | Postal code

Votre langue de correspondance : ☐ Français

Home address, if different from mailing address (Apt No – Street No Street name, RR)

Date of address change: Year | Month | Day

City | Province or territory | Postal code

Marital status – Select the box that applies to your marital status on the date you **became** a resident of Canada and enter the date this marital status began (leave the date blank if you have always been single). We define each marital status on page 3.

☐ Married ☐ Living common-law ☐ Widowed ☐ Divorced ☐ Separated ☐ Single   Since   Year | Month | Day

If your marital status has changed **since** you became a resident of Canada, select the box that applies to your new marital status and enter the date of this change:

☐ Married ☐ Living common-law ☐ Widowed ☐ Divorced ☐ Separated ☐ Single   Since   Year | Month | Day

Step 2 – Information about your spouse or common-law partner

First name | Last name | Social insurance number

Date of birth | Year | Month | Day | If your spouse or common-law partner's address is different than yours, enter it here; otherwise, their address will be updated to match the address indicated in Step 1

Step 3 – Your residency status

For more information, see "Who is considered a resident of Canada" on page 3.

A – Newcomer to Canada

	You			Your spouse or common-law partner		
	Year	Month	Day	Year	Month	Day
Enter the date you, or your spouse or common-law partner, became a resident of Canada						

B – Returning resident of Canada

	You			Your spouse or common-law partner		
Enter the Canadian province or territory in which you, or your spouse or common-law partner, resided before you cut your residential ties with Canada						
	Year	Month	Day	Year	Month	Day
Enter the date you, or your spouse or common-law partner, cut your residential ties with Canada (became a non-resident)						
	Year	Month	Day	Year	Month	Day
Enter the date you, or your spouse or common-law partner, re-established your residential ties with Canada (became a resident again)						

RC151 E (22) | (Ce formulaire est disponible en français.) | Page 1 of 4

Canadä

七、培訓學分(CTC)：

▶申請資格

1.加拿大稅務居民

2.加拿大培訓信用額度>0

> **Tips** ···

> 加拿大培訓信用額度(CTCL)：
>
> 每年，稅務居民提交報稅表格申請，CRA 審查通過後將您的CTCL增加 $ 250，一生最高可達 $ 5,000。

3.全年都是加拿大居民

4.年齡26~66歲

5.已支付培訓學費

6.學費符合抵免資格

   ✓ 入場費用

   ✓ 使用培訓需要設施使用費

   ✓ 考試費用

   ✓ 註冊費用

   ✓ 證書、文憑或學位費用

   ✓ 學費

▶申請表格

→申請培訓學分稅收抵免，需填寫表格5000-S11附表11。

T1-2021　　　　　　　　　　　　　　　　　　　　　Protected B when completed

Federal Tuition, Education, and　　　　　　　　Schedule 11
Textbook Amounts and Canada Training Credit

Only the student completes this schedule.

Complete this schedule to calculate your federal tuition, education, and textbook amounts and Canada training credit, your current-year unused tuition amount available to transfer to a designated individual, and your unused federal amount available to carry forward to a future year.

Use forms T2202, TL11A, and/or TL11C (or any other official tuition tax receipts) to complete this schedule. If you are transferring an amount, also use these forms to **designate** the individual you are transferring to and to **specify** the federal amount you are transferring.

Complete the provincial or territorial schedule (S11) to calculate your provincial or territorial amounts.

Attach a copy of this schedule to your paper return.

For more information, see Guide P105, Students and Income Tax.

Unused federal tuition, education, and textbook amounts from your 2020 notice of assessment or reassessment　　　　　　　　　　　　　　　　　　　　1

Eligible tuition fees paid to Canadian educational institutions for 2021 (1) **32000**　　2

If you are claiming the Canada training credit, continue on line 3.
If not, enter the amount from line 2 on line 7, and continue on line 8.

Amount from line 2 _____ × 50% =　　　　3

Your Canada training credit limit from your latest notice of assessment or reassessment　　4

Enter **whichever is less**: amount from line 3 or line 4.　　5

Enter the Canada training credit you are claiming (**cannot** be more than line 5).
Enter this amount on **line 45350** of your return.　**Canada training credit for 2021**　−　6

Available Canadian tuition amount for 2021:
Line 2 minus line 6　　　=　7

Eligible tuition fees paid to foreign educational institutions for 2021 **32001** +　8

Line 7 plus line 8　　=　▶　+　9

Total available tuition, education, and textbook amounts for 2021.
Line 1 plus line 9　　=　10

Enter the amount from line 26000 of your return on line 11 if it is **$49,020 or less**.
If it is **more than $49,020**, enter the result of the following calculation:
amount from line 73 of your return _____ ÷ 15% =　　11

Enter the amount from line 99 of your return.　−　12

Line 11 minus line 12 (if negative, enter "0")　=　13

Unused tuition, education, and textbook amounts claimed for 2021:
Enter **whichever is less**: amount from line 1 or line 13.　−　▶　14

Line 13 minus line 14　=　15

2021 tuition amount:
Enter **whichever is less**: amount from line 9 or line 15.　+　16

Line 14 plus line 16　　**Your tuition, education, and textbook**
Enter this amount on **line 32300** of your return.　**amounts claimed for 2021**　=　17

(1) The fees you paid to attend each institution must be **more than $100** to be eligible.

5000-S11 E (21)　　　　　　(Ce formulaire est disponible en français.)　　　　　Page 1 of 2

伍、加拿大所得稅率：

一、2022年聯邦稅率：

淨收入	稅率
未達$50,197	15%
超過$50,197~$100,392部分	20.5%
超過$100,392~$155,625部分	26%
超過$155,625~$221,708部分	29%
超過$221,708部分	33%

二、2022年省及地區稅率：

省和地區	淨收入	稅率
紐芬蘭-拉布拉多省 Newfoundland and Labrador	未達$39,147	8.7%
	未達$39,147	8.7%
	超過$39,147~$78,294部分	14.5%
	超過$78,294~$ 139,780部分	15.8%
	超過$139,780~$195,693部分	17.8%
	超過$195,693~$250,000部分	19.8%
	超過$250,000~$500,000部分	20.8%

省和地區	淨收入	稅率
	超過$500,000~$1,000,000部分	21.3%
	超過$1,000,000部分	21.8%
愛德華王子島 Prince Edward Island	未達$31,984	9.8%
	超過$31,984~$63,969部分	13.8%
	超過$69,969部分	16.7%
新斯科舍 Nova Scotia	未達$29,590	8.79%
	超過$29,590~$59,180部分	14.95%
	超過$59,180~$93,000部分	16.67%
	超過$93,000~$150,000部分	17.5%
	超過$150,000部分	21%
新不倫瑞克 New Brunswick	未達$44,887	9.4%
	超過$44,887~$89,775部分	14.82%
	超過$89,775~$145,955部分	16.52%
	超過$145,955~$166,280部分	17.84%
	超過$166,280部分	20.3%
魁北克省 Québec	未達$46,295	15%
	超過$46,295~$92,580部分	20%
	超過$92,580~$112,655部分	24%
	超過$112,655部分	25.75%

省和地區	淨收入	稅率
安大略 Ontario	未達$46,226	5.05%
	超過$46,226~$92,454部分	9.15%
	超過$92,454~$150,000部分	11.16%
	超過$150,000~$220,000部分	12.16%
	超過$220,000部分	13.16%
曼尼托巴 Manitoba	未達$34,431	10.8%
	超過$34,431~$74,416部分	12.75%
	超過$74,416部分	17.4%
薩斯喀徹溫 Saskatchewan	未達$46,773	10.5%
	超過$46,773~$133,638部分	12.5%
	超過$133,638部分	14.5%
艾伯塔 Alberta	未達$131,220	10%
	超過$131,220~$157,464部分	12%
	超過$157,464~$209,952部分	13%
	超過$209,952~$314,928部分	14%

省和地區	淨收入	稅率
	超過$314,928部分	15%
英屬哥倫比亞 British Columbia	未達$43,070	5.06%
	超過$43,070~$86,141部分	7.7%
	超過$86,141~$98,901部分	10.5%
	超過$98,901~$120,094部分	12.29%
	超過$120,094~$162,832部分	14.7%
	超過$162,832~$227,091部分	16.8%
	超過$227,091部分	20.5%
育空地區 Yukon	未達$50,197	6.4%
	超過$50,197~$100,392部分	9%
	超過$100,392~$155,625部分	10.9%
	超過$155,625~$500,000部分	12.8%
	超過$500,000部分	15%
西北領地 Northwest Territories	未達$45,462	5.9%
	超過$45,462~$90,927部分	8.6%

省和地區	淨收入	稅率
	超過$90,927~$147,826部分	12.2%
	超過$147,826部分	14.05%
紐納武特 Nunavut	未達$47,862	4%
	超過$47,862~$95,724部分	7%
	超過$95,724~$155,625部分	9%
	超過$155,625部分	11.5%

三、台灣與加拿大的稅率比較：

	綜所稅	營業稅	房產稅	資本利得稅	遺贈稅
台灣	5~40%	5%	房地合一 2.0(15~45%)	N/A	10~20%
加拿大	聯邦+省 BC: 20~53.5% Ontario: 20~46.16%	聯邦+省 聯邦:5% BC:7% Ontario: 8%	海外買家稅: 20% (購屋4年內成為居民可退還) 資本增值稅: 23% 移轉稅: 0.5~2%	資本利得 *50% 併入所得	無遺產稅 (由資本利得稅取代)

陸、申報表格：

一般來說您會在 2 月底前收到您的大部分稅單。但是，您可能要到 3 月底才能收到 T3稅單。您通常會收到一式三份的副本，一份附在您的加拿大聯邦納稅申報表上，一份附在您的省或地區報稅表上，另一份自己留存。如果您不只一份工作，您也可能會收到多張稅單。以下介紹常見稅單種類：

▶T4稅單

T4稅單是從雇主那裏收到的文件，向加拿大稅務局（CRA）證明您在上一年度獲得多少薪資收入，包括工資、獎金、加班費、小費、佣金、應稅津貼等等。

▶截止日期

T4稅單必須在課稅年度終結後的二月份的最後一天前發出。 例如，您應該在2022年2月28日之前收到2021年收入的T4稅單。

▶T4A稅單

T4A稅單是指養老金、退休金、年金和其他收入表，由雇主、受託人、遺產執行人或清算人、養老金管理機構編制和發布，用以告訴您和加拿大稅務局(CRA)您在這個稅務年度這些類型的收入和扣除的所得稅額。

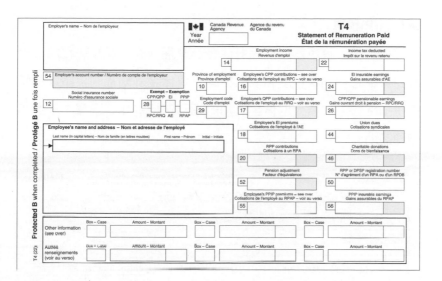

▶T4A(OAS)稅單

T4A(OAS)稅單或老年保障聲明，以告訴您和加拿大稅務局(CRA)
您在納稅年度內收到的多少老年保障收入以及所得稅額被扣除。

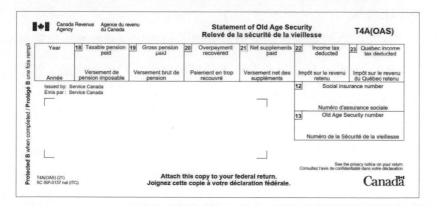

▶T4A(P)稅單

T4A（P）稅單或加拿大退休金計劃福利表，通知您和加拿大稅務機構您在納稅年度領取的加拿大退休金計劃福利金額以及所得稅扣除額。加拿大退休金計劃的福利包括退休、遺囑、子女和喪葬補助。

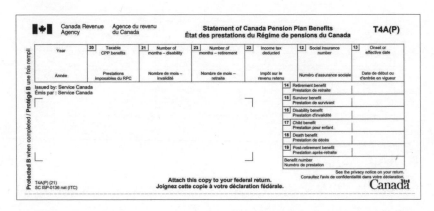

▶T4E稅單

T4E稅單是就業保險及其他福利表，以告知您和加拿大稅務局（CRA）在前一個納稅年度支付給您的就業保險福利總額，包括所得稅扣除以及任何超額付款。

Canada Revenue Agency / Agence du revenu du Canada	T4E	Statement of Employment Insurance and Other Benefits État des prestations d'assurance-emploi et autres prestations	Protected B / Protégé B when completed / une fois rempli

| Year / Année | 7 Repayment rate
Taux de remboursement | 14 Total benefits paid
Prestations totales versées | 15 Regular and other benefits paid
Prestations régulières et autres prestations versées | 17 Employment benefits and support measures paid
Prestations d'emploi et mesures de soutien versées | 20 Taxable tuition assistance
Aide visant les frais de scolarité imposables | 21 Non-taxable tuition assistance
Aide visant les frais de scolarité non imposables |

| 22 Income tax deducted
Impôt sur le revenu retenu | 23 Quebec income tax deducted
Impôt du Québec sur le revenu retenu | 12 Social insurance number
Numéro d'assurance sociale |

Other information (see the next page) – Autres renseignements (à la page suivante)

Box /Case	Amount / Montant	Box /Case	Amount / Montant

Recipient's name and address – Nom et adresse du bénéficiaire

Payer's name – Nom du payeur

Attach this copy to your federal return
Joignez cette copie à votre déclaration fédérale

Canadä

T4E (22)

▶T4RSP稅單

T4RSP稅單或RRSP收入聲明是由金融機構編制和發布的，以告訴您和加拿大稅務局（CRA）您在給定納稅年度從RRSP退出或收到多少錢，以及扣除了多少稅金。

Canada Revenue Agency / Agence du revenu du Canada	Statement of RRSP Income État du revenu provenant d'un REER	T4RSP

| Year / Année | 16 Annuity payments
Paiements de rente | 18 Refund of premiums
Remboursement de primes | 20 Refund of unused contributions
Remboursement des cotisations inutilisées | 22 Withdrawal and commutation payments
Retrait et paiements de conversion | 25 LLP withdrawal
Retrait REEP | 26 Amounts deemed received on deregistration
Montants réputés reçus lors de l'annulation de l'enregistrement |

| 28 Other income or deductions
Autres revenus ou déductions | 30 Income tax deducted
Impôt sur le revenu retenu | 34 Amounts deemed received on death
Montants réputés reçus au décès | 37 Advanced Life Deferred Annuity purchase
Achat de rente viagère différée à un âge avancé | 27 HBP withdrawal
Retrait RAP | 35 Transfers on breakdown of marriage or common-law part.
Transferts après rupture du mariage ou de l'union de fait |

Recipient's name and address – Nom et adresse du bénéficiaire

Last name (print) Nom de famille (en lettres moulées)	First name Prénom	Initials Initiales

24 Contributor spouse or common-law partner Époux ou conjoint de fait cotisant	Yes / Oui ☐ No / Non ☐	36 Spouse's or common-law partner's social insurance number Numéro d'assurance sociale de l'époux ou du conjoint de fait

12 Social insurance number* Numéro d'assurance sociale*	14 Contract number Numéro de contrat

60 Name of payer (issuer) of plan – Nom du payeur (émetteur) du régime

61 Account number Numéro de compte	40 Tax-paid amount Montant libéré d'impôt

See the privacy notice on your return
Consultez l'avis de confidentialité dans votre déclaration

T4RSP (21)

*If your social insurance number is not shown, see the back of this slip.
*Si votre numéro d'assurance sociale n'est pas indiqué, lisez le verso de ce feuillet.

Protected B when completed / **Protégé B** une fois rempli

▶T5稅單

T5稅單是指投資收益表，由支付利息、股息的單位編制和發布的，以告訴您和加拿大稅務局(CRA)您在納稅年度獲得多少投資收入。包括大部分股息、特許權使用費、銀行存款利息等等。

截止日期

T5稅單必須在2月的最後一天發布，即T5稅率適用年度的隔年2月。例如，您應該在2022年2月28日之前收到2021年收入的T5稅單。

◆ Canada Revenue Agency Agence du revenu du Canada	**T5**	Statement of Investment Income État des revenus de placement		Year Année	Protected B / Protégé B when completed / une fois rempli
Dividends from Canadian corporations – Dividendes de sociétés canadiennes			Federal credit – Crédit fédéral		
24 Actual amount of eligible dividends	25 Taxable amount of eligible dividends	26 Dividend tax credit for eligible dividends	13 Interest from Canadian sources	18 Capital gains dividends	
Montant réel des dividendes déterminés	Montant imposable des dividendes déterminés	Crédit d'impôt pour dividendes déterminés	Intérêts de source canadienne	Dividendes sur gains en capital	
10 Actual amount of dividends other than eligible dividends	11 Taxable amount of dividends other than eligible dividends	12 Dividend tax credit for dividends other than eligible dividends	21 Report Code	22 Recipient identification number	23 Recipient type
Montant réel des dividendes autres que des dividendes déterminés	Montant imposable des dividendes autres que des dividendes déterminés	Crédit d'impôt pour dividendes autres que des dividendes déterminés	Code du feuillet	Numéro d'identification du bénéficiaire	Type de bénéficiaire
Other information (see the back) Autres renseignements (lisez le dos)	Box / Case Amount / Montant		Box / Case Amount / Montant	Box / Case Amount / Montant	
Recipient's name (last name first) and address – Nom, prénom et adresse du bénéficiaire			Payer's name and address – Nom et adresse du payeur		
Currency and identification codes Codes de devise et d'identification ▶	27 Foreign currency Devises étrangères	28 Transit – Succursale	29 Recipient account number Numéro de compte du bénéficiaire	For information, see the back. Pour obtenir des renseignements, lisez le dos.	
See the privacy notice on your return./ Consultez l'avis de confidentialité dans votre déclaration. T5 (09/21)					

▶T3稅單

T3稅單指信託收入，由財務管理人員和受託人編制並發布，以告訴您和加拿大稅務局(CRA)您從共同基金的投資中獲得多少收入、來自商業收入信託或納稅年度房地產的收入。

截止日期

與大多數其他稅單不同，T3稅單的截止日期為稅務年度隔年三月份的最後一天。例如，您應該在2022年3月31日之前收到2021年收入的T3稅單。

▶T2202稅單

T2202是指加拿大大學的學費證明，用以證明您有繳納學費，可以做為退稅用途。

第二節 福利

壹、育兒福利：

一、加拿大兒童福利 (CCB)：

　　加拿大兒童福利金（Canada Child Care Benefit）也被俗稱為「牛奶金」。是加拿大政府按月支付給符合資格申請人的福利金，該福利金免稅，目的是用以幫助養育18歲以下加拿大兒童成長費用。

▶**申請資格**

✓ 撫養未滿18歲兒童

✓ 申請人是加拿人稅務居民

✓ 配偶是公民或永久居民

▶**申請金額**

撫養子女數	家庭年收入	每年可領取金額(每個小孩)
1個	低於 $ 32,797	6歲以下：$ 6,997 6~17歲：$5,903
	$ 32,797~$71,060	6歲以下：最低$ 4,319 6~17歲：最低$3,225

撫養子女數	家庭年收入	每年可領取金額(每個小孩)
1個	超過 $ 71,060	6歲以下：最高$ 4,319 6~17歲：最高$3,225
2個	低於 $ 32,797	6歲以下：$ 6,997 6~17歲：$5,903
	$ 32,797~$71,060	6歲以下：最低$ 4,414 6~17歲：最低$3,320
	超過 $ 71,060	6歲以下：最高$ 4,414 6~17歲：最高$3,320
3個	低於 $ 32,797	6歲以下：$ 6,997 6~17歲：$5,903
	$ 32,797~$71,060	6歲以下：最低$ 4,574 6~17歲：最低$3,480
	超過 $ 71,060	6歲以下：最高$ 4,574 6~17歲：最高$3,480
4個	低於 $ 32,797	6歲以下：$ 6,997 6~17歲：$5,903
	$ 32,797~$71,060	6歲以下：最低$ 4,797 6~17歲：最低$3,703
	超過 $ 71,060	6歲以下：最高$ 4,797 6~17歲：最高$3,703

▶申請表格

➡申請加拿大兒童福利CCB需填寫表格RC66

■◆■ Canada Revenue Agency	Agence du revenu du Canada		**Protected B** when completed

Canada Child Benefits Application
includes federal, provincial, and territorial programs

Find out if this form is for you

Fill out this form to apply for the Canada child benefit and register your children for the goods and services tax/harmonized sales tax (GST/HST) credit, the climate action incentive payment (CAIP) and related federal, provincial, or territorial programs the Canada Revenue Agency (CRA) administers. You can also use this form if you started a shared-custody situation for one or more children.

Do not fill out this form if you already applied using My Account on the CRA website or when you registered the birth of your newborn with your province or territory (except Yukon and Nunavut).

Who should fill out this form

The person who is **primarily responsible** for the care and upbringing of the child should apply (see "Primarily responsible for the care and upbringing of the child" on page 3).

When a child resides with a female parent in the home, the female parent is usually considered to be primarily responsible for the child and should apply. However, if the child's other parent is primarily responsible, they should apply and attach a signed letter from the female parent stating that the other parent with whom she resides is primarily responsible for all the children in the home. If the child lives with same-sex parents, only one parent should apply for all the children in the home.

For more information

For more information on the Canada child benefit, including eligibility requirements, go to canada.ca/cra-benefits, see Booklet T4114, Canada Child Benefit, or call 1-800-387-1193. From outside Canada or the United States, call 1 613 940 8495. We accept collect calls by automated response.

Step 1 – Your information

Social insurance number (SIN): | | | | | | | | |

If you do not have a SIN, see Booklet T4114, Canada Child Benefit, under "How to apply."

First name: _____

Last name: _____

Date of birth: | | | | | |
            Year Month Day

Your language of correspondence: ☐ English ☐ Français

Phone numbers: Home: _____ Work: _____ Ext: _____ Cell: _____

Step 2 – Your address

Mailing address

Apt. No. – Street No., Street name, PO Box, RR: _____

City: _____

Province or territory (or country if outside Canada): _____

Postal or ZIP code: _____

Have you moved from a different province or territory within the last 12 months? ☐ Yes ☐ No

If **yes**, enter the previous province or territory and the date you moved: _____ Date: | | | | | |
                                       Year Month Day

Home address ☐ Same as mailing address

Apt. No. – Street No., Street name, RR: _____

City: _____

Province or territory (or country if outside Canada): _____

Postal or ZIP code: _____

二、加拿大教育儲蓄補助金 (CESG)：

加拿大教育儲蓄補助金 (CESG) 是加拿大政府提供到註冊教育儲蓄計劃 (RESP)中的資金。這筆錢有助於支付孩子高中畢業後的全日制或非全日制學習費用。

▶ 申請資格

✓ 加拿大居民

✓ 年滿17歲

✓ 必須向RESP存款才能獲得CESG

▶ 申請金額

CESG 提供註冊教育儲蓄計劃 (RESP) 存款的 20%，最高 $ 2,500。意指 CESG 每年最多可以為 RESP 增加 $ 500。一個孩子終身可以獲得的最高 CESG 金額為 $ 7, 200。

三、註冊教育儲蓄計劃 (RESP)：

註冊教育儲蓄計劃（RESP）是一項政府註冊的儲蓄計劃，可以幫助您儲蓄子女未來的高等教育費用。當您的子女被符合資格的高等教育機構錄取時，您就可以為教育用途提取資金，使用這些資金發放的款項被稱為教育補助金 (EAP)。存款無法作為減稅用途，但是帳戶內累積的利息收入不需課稅，未來連本帶利用做子女的教育費。當子女收到教育費時，須申報收入課稅，但是因為子女的所得稅率通常比父母低，因此可以達到分散收入的目的。

▶ **申請資格**

任何人都可以為孩子開設 RESP 帳戶，包括父母、監護人、祖父母、其他親戚或朋友。您也可以替自己開設RESP帳戶儲蓄。

▶ **可提款項目**

✓ 學費　　✓ 書籍費　　✓ 交通費　　✓ 住宿費

▶ **存款限額**

沒有年度存款限制，但是有終身存款 $ 50,000限額，每年依存款額度額外發放20%助學金，雖然可以一次就存滿限額，但是為了獲得每年最多 $ 500的助學金(終身最多 $ 7200)，最佳存款方式為每年最少存款 $ 2,500，持續至少15年。

	第一年就存滿 $ 50,000	第一年存款 $15,000，之後每年存款 $ 2500持續存滿15年
終身存款	$ 50,000	15,000+2,500*14=$ 50,000
CESG助學金	$ 500	500*14+200= $ 7,200 (最高終身限額)

▶ 種類

合資性

由眾多存款者將資金匯集到政府指定的教育基金，投資方式較為保守，並且需指定受益人名字。

獨資性

由銀行、互惠基金或財務機構提供給單一客戶的儲蓄計劃，投資方式較為靈活，可依照客戶需求調整，可有多位有血緣關係的受益人。

貳、就業福利：

一、就業保險 (EI)：

加拿大是世界上擁有最全面的福利制度的國家之一，各種職業都有許多福利，以確保每個人都有權利在勞動力市場上獲得工作或擁有一技之長。就業保險EI是最常見的一種，政府為那些非自願而失去工作的工人提供就業保險EI，例如：季節性因素、公司大規模裁員而失去工作、工作市場短缺、以前的工作場所關閉、有技術但找不到工作等等原因。

▶ **申請資格**

1.受僱於可提供保險的工作，至少工作滿420小時。

2.非自願失去工作

3.過去52週至少連續7天沒有工作沒有薪水

4.有就業意願並積極尋找工作

▶ **標準福利**

✓ 可獲得平均每周收入的55%(最高每周 $ 638)

✓ 可領取最長45周

▶ **醫療福利**

當您因生病無法工作時，且每周正常收入減少40%以上持續至少1周，則可以持醫生開立的診斷證明申請EI醫療福利津貼，最多可以獲得15周收入55%的醫療津貼。

▶ **生育津貼**

當您因為懷孕而無法工作時，且每周正常收入減少40%以上持續至少1周，則最早可以在預產期或分娩日期前 12 週開始領取生育福利津貼，最多可以獲得15周收入55%的生育津貼。

▶育兒福利

當您因為育兒而無法工作時，可以選擇申請一般育兒福利或是延長育兒福利，一般育兒福利最長可以領取52周，每周最多$638；延長育兒福利最長可領取78周，每周最多$383。

▶看護福利

當您因為有需要照護的家庭成員而無法工作時，依被照顧人的類別可申請最長35周的看護福利津貼，類別分為以下三種：

被照顧人	最長可申請週數
18歲以下兒童	35週
18歲以上重病或重傷者	15週
臨終者	26週

二、加拿大社會福利金（Social Welfare）：

社會福利金又稱作失業救濟金，主要針對長期失業人士所提供的福利，使他們雖然沒有工作，還是能維持最低生活水準，福利包含日常生活所需、住所、飲食、醫藥費等等，並提供職業培訓以協助其就業順利。

▶申請資格

✓ 沒有收入

✓ 存款 $ 1,000以下

▶可申請金額

■ 單身：一個月 $ 500~ $ 700

■ 家庭：一個月 $ 1,000~ $ 1,300

參、置產福利：

一、購房者計劃 (Home Buyers' Plan,HBP)：

購房者計劃 (HBP) 是一項允許您從註冊退休儲蓄計劃 (RRSP) 中提取資金的計劃，以便為自己或相關的殘障人士購買或建造符合條件的房屋，並允許您在 15 年內償還提取的資金。

▶申請資格

✓ 首次購房者　　✓ 加拿大居民　　✓ 與殘障人士合約書

✓ 購買或建造之房屋1年內為主要居住地

▶提款限額

HBP 提款限額為 $ 35,000，夫妻共可以提款 $ 70,000。

▶申請表格

➡申請購房者計劃HBP需填寫表格T1036請求從 RRSP 中提取資金。

Protected B when completed

Home Buyers' Plan (HBP)
Request to Withdraw Funds from an RRSP

Use this form to make a withdrawal from your registered retirement savings plan (RRSP) under the Home Buyers' Plan (HBP). Fill out Part A of Area 1 to determine if you are eligible to make a withdrawal from your RRSP under the HBP. Although some conditions may apply to another person in certain situations, you (the participant) are responsible for making sure that all the conditions are met. For more information about the HBP, including changes to the rules for first-time home buyers, go to canada.ca/home-buyers-plan. Generally, you must receive all your HBP withdrawals in the same calendar year. The maximum you can withdraw is $35,000. Fill out Area 1 and give the form to your financial institution who must fill out Area 2. Keep a copy of the completed form for your records.

Area 1 – To be filled out by the participant

Part A – Fill out the following questionnaire to determine if you can make a withdrawal from your RRSP under the HBP

1. Are you a resident of Canada?	☐ Yes – Go to question 2.	☐ No – You cannot make an HBP withdrawal.
2. Has the person buying or building a **qualifying home** * entered into a **written agreement** * to do so?	☐ Yes – Go to question 3a.	☐ No – You cannot make an HBP withdrawal.
3a). Have you ever, before this year, withdrawn funds from your RRSP under the HBP to buy or build a qualifying home?	☐ Yes – Go to question 3b.	☐ No – Go to question 4.
3b). Are you making this request in January as part of the participation you began last year?	☐ Yes – Go to question 4.	☐ No – Go to question 3c.
3c). Was your repayable balance from your previous HBP participation **zero** on January 1 of this year?	☐ Yes – Go to question 4.	☐ No – You cannot make an HBP withdrawal.
4. Do you intend to occupy the qualifying home that you are buying or building as your principal place of residence no later than one year after buying or building it? If you are acquiring the home for a **related person** * with a disability or helping a related person with a disability acquire the home, you must intend that the related person with a disability occupy the home as their principal place of residence no later than one year after buying or building it.	☐ Yes – Go to question 5.	☐ No – You cannot make an HBP withdrawal.
5. Has the person who is buying or building the **qualifying home** or their spouse or common-law partner owned the **qualifying home** more than 30 days before receiving this withdrawal?	☐ Yes – You cannot make an HBP withdrawal. **However**, if you are making this withdrawal **after 2019** to acquire the interest or right of your separated spouse or common-law partner in the home, go to question 8a) to confirm your eligibility.	☐ No – Go to question 6a.
6a). Are you a person with a disability?	☐ Yes – You are eligible (fill out Part B).	☐ No – Go to question 6b.
6b). Are you withdrawing funds from your RRSP to buy or build a qualifying home for a related person with a disability or to help such a person buy or build a qualifying home?	☐ Yes – You are eligible (fill out Part B).	☐ No – Go to question 7.
7. At any time during the period beginning January 1 of the fourth year before the year of the withdrawal and ending 31 days before the date of the withdrawal, did you or your spouse or common-law partner own a home that you occupied as an individual with a marital status of single, or with that individual while you were spouses or common-law partners?	☐ Yes – You are not considered a **first-time home buyer** *, and you cannot make a HBP withdrawal. **However**, if you are making this withdrawal **after 2019** and experienced a breakdown of marriage or common-law partnership, go to question 8a) to confirm your eligibility.	☐ No – You are eligible (fill out Part B).

Notes

1. **Qualifying home** – a qualifying home is a housing unit located in Canada. This includes existing homes and those being constructed. Single-family homes, semi-detached homes, townhouses, mobile homes, condominium units, and apartments in duplexes, triplexes, fourplexes, or apartment buildings all qualify. A share in a co-operative housing corporation that entitles you to possess, and gives you an equity interest in a housing unit located in Canada, also qualifies. However, a share that only provides you with a right to tenancy in the housing unit does not qualify. For condominium units, you are considered to own the unit the day you are entitled to immediate vacant possession of it.

2. **Written agreement** – a written agreement must include the date the agreement was signed, the address of the qualifying home and the closing date.

3. **Related person** – a person connected to you by a blood relationship, marriage, common-law partnership, or adoption (legal or in fact). For more information, see Income Tax Folio, S1-F5-C1, Related Person and Dealing at Arm's Length.

4. **First-time home buyer** – you are considered a first-time home buyer if, in the period that begins on January 1 of the fourth year before the year you withdraw funds from your RRSP, and ends 31 days before the date you withdraw the funds, you did not occupy a home that you owned, or one that your current spouse or common-law partner owned. For example, if you are withdrawing the funds on July 31, 2021, the period is from January 1, 2017 to June 30, 2021.

(Continued on next page)

T1036 E (21)   (Ce formulaire disponible en français.)   Page 1 of 2   **Canada**

二、反向房屋貸款(Reverse Mortgage)：

對於擁有房屋的退休人士來說，反向房屋貸款也可以算是一筆退休收入，透過將房屋抵押給金融機構，來獲得貸款支應退休費用，一般來說可以貸到房屋價值約10~40%左右，唯一規定是必須年滿62歲才能申請，年紀越大可以貸款金額越多，屋主不必每月還款，只須待未來房屋出售時再一併償還本金及利息即可。

肆、退休福利：

一、加拿大退休金計劃 (Canada Pension Plan,CPP)：

加拿大退休金計劃為加拿大的確定給付制退休金制度，幾乎所有加拿大民眾都包含在此制度中，提撥部分由雇主跟員工分別提撥50%的費率，給付項目包括各式退休金給付、傷殘津貼、遺屬津貼，類似於我國勞保。

▶領取時間

標準領取養老金的年齡為65歲，最早可以60歲開始領取，則每月減少0.6%金額，最多減少36%養老金；最晚可以70歲領取，則每月增加0.7%金額，最多增加42%養老金。

▶領取金額

可領取金額取決於開始領取的年齡、提撥了多長時間以及提撥期間平均收入而定，最高每月可領取$1253.59。亦可將退休金分配最多一半給配偶，達到分散收入的目的。

二、加拿大退休金計劃 (CPP) 殘疾福利：

殘疾福利金是加拿大退休金計劃的其中一種，是按月發給曾提撥退休金的殘疾人士及其要撫養的子女，金額包括殘疾福利金（Disability Benefits）及子女津貼（Children's Benefits）。

▶申請資格
- ✓ 未滿65歲　　✓ 生理上或心理上殘疾
- ✓ 未領取CPP退休金

▶子女津貼
- ✓ 18歲以下子女　　✓ 18~25歲就學中子女

▶可領取金額

福利名稱	資格	每月最高金額
CPP殘疾福利	未滿65歲且未領CPP退休金	$1464.83
CPP退休後殘疾福利	60~65歲且已領CPP退休金	$524.64
CPP子女津貼	18歲以下或18~25歲就學中子女	$264.53

三、老人年金(Old Age Security ,OAS)：

　　OAS是加拿大政府按月支付給65歲以上，屬於加拿大公民或合法居民的老年人福利。要獲得最高的OAS金額，則需在加拿大居住了40年以上（18歲以後）。

▶申請資格

　　✓ 18歲以後在加拿大境內住滿10年

　　✓ 年滿65歲(2023年4月開始須年滿67歲)

　　✓ 加拿大公民或永久居民

　　✓ 居住在加拿大

▶申請金額

　　金額的大小與住在加拿大的時間有關，18歲以後在加拿大境內住滿40年，65~74歲每月可以領取最高金額 $ 685.5，75歲以上每月可以領取最高金額 $ 754.05，若是僅住滿10年，則依比例計算領取1/4金額；住滿 20 年以上，則可以在加拿大以外的地區領取老人年金。

　　若是選擇延遲領取養老金，最長可以延遲5年至70歲領取，每月可增加0.6%，5年最多可以增加36%。

　　年收入在 $ 80,000以下可以領取最多金額；年收入在 $ 80,000~ $ 130,000之間則隨著收入增加而遞減；年收入超過 $ 130,000則無法領取養老金。

▶ 申請表格

➡ 申請老人年金OAS需填寫表格ISP3550

Service Canada

PROTECTED B (when completed)

Application for the Old Age Security Pension and the Guaranteed Income Supplement

Information about this application

Old Age Security (OAS) is a monthly payment available to seniors aged 65 or over who meet the legal status and residence requirements. If Service Canada has enough information to determine that you are eligible to receive the OAS pension, you will receive a letter to inform you that your pension will be paid to you automatically when you reach age 65. If you did not receive a letter, complete and submit this application to apply. Also use this application to apply for the Guaranteed Income Supplement (GIS), a non-taxable amount added to the OAS pension. The GIS amount depends on your marital status and annual net income. Each section of this application has information and instructions to assist you:

- A. Personal information
- B. Applying for the Old Age Security pension
- C. Applying for the Guaranteed Income Supplement
- D. Payment information
- E. Benefits from other countries
- F. Declaration and signature
- G. Terms and Conditions/Privacy Notice Statement

⚠ When you see this symbol, read the information provided.

(?) For information about the OAS program, visit Canada.ca/OAS or call Service Canada at 1-800-277-9914.

Section A Personal information

A1 Social Insurance Number		A2 Preferred language ○ English ○ French
A3 Optional ○ Mr. ○ Mrs. ○ Ms. ○ Miss	A4 First name	Middle name	Last name(s)
A5 Date of birth (YYYY-MM-DD)	Last name at birth (if different from above)	

⚠ You do not need to provide proof of your date of birth when you apply. Service Canada may contact you to ask for proof later.

A6 Home address (no., street, apt., RR)

City/Town	Province/Territory	Country	Postal code
Telephone number		Alternate telephone number	

A7 Mailing address if different from above (no., street, apt., PO box, RR)

City/Town	Province/Territory	Country	Postal code

Service Canada delivers Employment and Social Development Canada programs and services for the Government of Canada

SC ISP-3550 (2022-10-01) E 　　1 / 9 　　Disponible en français

Canada

四、保證收入補助金 (GIS)：

GIS是OAS計劃的一部分，只有領取養老金(OAS)的人才可有資格申請GIS，是提供給低收入老年人的一種收入補助。

▶申請資格

✓ 年滿65歲

✓ 居住在加拿大

✓ 已經在領取老人年金OAS

✓ 收入低於GIS標準

婚姻狀況	家庭年收入	每月最多可領取金額
單身	低於 $ 20,784	$ 1,023.88
配偶有領取OAS	低於 $ 27,456	$ 616.31
配偶有領取60-64津貼	低於 $ 38,448	$ 616.31
配偶沒有領取OAS	低於 $ 49,824	$ 1,023.88

▶申請表格

➡申請保證收入補助金GIS需填寫表格ISP3550

	Service Canada		PROTECTED B (when completed)

Application for the Old Age Security Pension and the Guaranteed Income Supplement

Information about this application

Old Age Security (OAS) is a monthly payment available to seniors aged 65 or over who meet the legal status and residence requirements. If Service Canada has enough information to determine that you are eligible to receive the OAS pension, you will receive a letter to inform you that your pension will be paid to you automatically when you reach age 65. If you did not receive a letter, complete and submit this application to apply. Also use this application to apply for the Guaranteed Income Supplement (GIS), a non-taxable amount added to the OAS pension. The GIS amount depends on your marital status and annual net income. Each section of this application has information and instructions to assist you:

A. Personal information

B. Applying for the Old Age Security pension

C. Applying for the Guaranteed Income Supplement

D. Payment information

E. Benefits from other countries

F. Declaration and signature

G. Terms and Conditions/Privacy Notice Statement

⚠ When you see this symbol, read the information provided.

(?) For information about the OAS program, visit Canada.ca/OAS or call Service Canada at 1-800-277-9914.

Section A Personal information

A1 Social Insurance Number		A2 Preferred language ○ English ○ French	
A3 Optional ○ Mr. ○ Mrs. ○ Ms. ○ Miss	A4 First name	Middle name	Last name(s)
A5 Date of birth (YYYY-MM-DD)	Last name at birth (if different from above)		

⚠ You do not need to provide proof of your date of birth when you apply. Service Canada may contact you to ask for proof later.

A6 Home address (no., street, apt., RR)

City/Town	Province/Territory	Country	Postal code
Telephone number		Alternate telephone number	

A7 Mailing address if different from above (no., street, apt., PO box, RR)

City/Town	Province/Territory	Country	Postal code

Service Canada delivers Employment and Social Development Canada programs and services for the Government of Canada

SC ISP-3550 (2022-10-01) E　　　　　1 / 9　　　　Disponible en français　　　　Canada

五、保證收入補助金 (GIS) -配偶津貼：

這是OAS計劃下的福利，支付給年齡在60歲至64歲之間的低收入老年人，一旦年滿65歲停止，即轉為領取老人年金OAS，屬於一種臨時性的福利。

▶申請資格

✓ 年齡60~64歲(2023年4月之後，年齡須介於62~64歲之間)

✓ 18歲以後在加拿大住滿10年

✓ 配偶是OAS和GIS的受益人

✓ 收入低於GIS標準

婚姻狀況	家庭年收入	每月最多可領取金額
配偶或伴侶領取OAS和GIS全額補助金	低於 $ 38,448	$ 1,301.81

▶申請表格

➡申請保證收入補助金GIS-配偶津貼需填寫表格ISP3008

<table>
<tr><td colspan="2">**Service Canada**</td><td colspan="2">**PROTECTED B (when completed)**
Personal Information Bank ESDC PPU 116</td></tr>
</table>

Application for the Allowance or Allowance for the Survivor
Under the Old Age Security Program

1. Social Insurance Number	2. ⚪ Mr. ⚪ Mrs. ⚪ Ms. ⚪ Miss	**Your first name, initial and last name**

3. **Name at birth** (If different from above)	4. **Date of birth** (YYYY-MM-DD)	**FOR OFFICE USE ONLY** Age established

Important: You do not need to provide proof of birth with your application. However, the Old Age Security program has the right to request proof of birth at any time, when deemed necessary.

5. **Country of birth** (If born in Canada, indicate province or territory)	6. **Preferred language for correspondence** ⚪ English ⚪ French

7a. Home address

No., Street, Apt. No., R.R.	City, town or village
Province or territory	Country	Postal code

Telephone number during the day

7b. Mailing address (if different from home address)

No., Street, Apt. No., P.O. Box, R.R.	City, town or village
Province or territory	Country	Postal code

8. Payment information

Direct deposit in Canada:

Complete the boxes below with your banking information.

Branch Number (5 digits)	Institution Number (3 digits)	Account Number (maximum of 12 digits)

Name(s) on the account	Telephone number of your financial institution

Direct deposit outside Canada:

For direct deposit outside Canada, please contact us at 1-800-277-9914 from the United States and at 613-957-1954 from all other countries (collect calls accepted). The form and a list of countries where direct deposit service is available can be found at **www.directdeposit.gc.ca**.

Service Canada delivers Employment and Social Development Canada programs and services for the Government of Canada

SC ISP-3008 (2016-05-02) E   1 / 4   Disponible en français   **Canadä**

六、保證收入補助金 (GIS) -遺孀：

這是OAS計劃下的福利，支付給年齡在60歲至64歲之間的遺孀，一旦年滿65歲停止，即轉為領取老人年金OAS，屬於一種臨時性的福利。

▶申請資格

✓ 年齡60~64歲(2023年4月之後，年齡須介於62~64歲之間)

✓ 配偶是OAS和GIS的受益人

✓ 曾經居住加拿大超過10年

✓ 配偶已過世且未再婚

✓ 收入低於GIS標準

婚姻狀況	家庭年收入	每月最多可領取金額
遺孀	低於 $ 27,984	$ 1,551.85

▶申請表格

➡申請保證收入補助金GIS-遺孀津貼需填寫表格ISP3008

Service Canada

PROTECTED B (when completed)
Personal Information Bank ESDC PPU 116

Application for the Allowance or Allowance for the Survivor
Under the Old Age Security Program

1. Social Insurance Number

2. ○ Mr. ○ Mrs. ○ Ms. ○ Miss

Your first name, initial and last name

3. Name at birth (If different from above)

4. Date of birth (YYYY-MM-DD)

FOR OFFICE USE ONLY
Age established

Important: You do not need to provide proof of birth with your application. However, the Old Age Security program has the right to request proof of birth at any time, when deemed necessary.

5. Country of birth (If born in Canada, indicate province or territory)

6. Preferred language for correspondence

○ English ○ French

7a. Home address

No., Street, Apt. No., R.R.

City, town or village

Province or territory

Country

Postal code

Telephone number during the day

7b. Mailing address (if different from home address)

No., Street, Apt. No., P.O. Box, R.R.

City, town or village

Province or territory

Country

Postal code

8. Payment Information

Direct deposit in Canada:

Complete the boxes below with your banking information.

Branch Number
(5 digits)

Institution Number
(3 digits)

Account Number
(maximum of 12 digits)

Name(s) on the account

Telephone number of your financial institution

Direct deposit outside Canada:

For direct deposit outside Canada, please contact us at 1-800-277-9914 from the United States and at 613-957-1954 from all other countries (collect calls accepted). The form and a list of countries where direct deposit service is available can be found at **www.directdeposit.gc.ca**.

Service Canada delivers Employment and Social Development Canada programs and services for the Government of Canada

SC ISP-3008 (2016-05-02) E   1 / 4   Disponible en français

Canada

七、註冊退休儲蓄計劃 (RRSP)：

　　註冊退休儲蓄計劃 (RRSP) 是一種在加拿大政府註冊的儲蓄計劃，鼓勵您做儲蓄以保障您的退休生活。此外，當您向RRSP存款時，您的資金可享受「稅收優惠」，這代表在您存款的那一年，存款可以免稅，但是每年存款額度是有限的。隨後，只要這筆資金保留在RRSP內，RRSP持有的投資在取款之前賺取的任何投資收入都可以免稅，延遲到取款時再列為收入。而由於退休後提領時的收入可能比在職時少很多，因此可以適用較低的稅率，就可以為您省較多稅款。至於帳戶內的可以隨個人決定如何使用，並無限制。可以持續存款至年滿71歲，若是配偶尚未年滿71歲，則可以存款至配偶的RRSP帳戶內，達到分散收入的目的。

▶申請資格

　　年滿18歲以上加拿大居民

▶存款限額

　　若是沒有其他公司註冊的退休計畫，則限額為去年勞工收入的18%或是以下限額(取低者)。

年度	限額
2022年	$ 29,210
2021年	$ 27,830

年度	限額
2020年	$ 27,230
2019年	$ 26,500
2018年	$ 26,230
2017年	$ 26,010

▶超額罰款

若是存入RRSP帳戶超過年度限額，會有每月1%的超額罰款，但是超額在$ 2,000以下不罰，因此可以在RRSP帳戶內額外存入$ 2,000以下的存款，比起存在銀行帳戶內，存入RRSP可以暫時免稅。

▶提領方式

一次領取

➡一次領取帳戶中所有金額，但是提取金額全數須列報當年度收入報稅，因此一次領取可能需要支付最高所得稅稅率。

年金領取

➡將帳戶中金額轉移到財務機構，依照個人需求分為10年期、20年期或是終身年金，期限越短，每次可提取金額越多，每年提取金額須列報收入報稅。

註冊退休入息基金Registered Retirement Income Fund (RRIF)

➡ 將帳戶中金額轉移到另一個註冊退休入息基金(RRIF)帳戶，這是一個不能存款的帳戶，一旦轉入後須依照政府規定每年領取金額。

伍、其他福利：

一、註冊殘障儲蓄計劃（RDSP）：

註冊殘障儲蓄計劃（RDSP）是加拿大政府主導的一項儲蓄計劃，透過每年持續的存款並領取補助金，直至年滿60歲得以提款，能幫助殘障人士建立長遠的經濟保障。這項儲蓄計劃能使他們獲得收人補助、擁有房屋以及生活品質的提升。

▶申請資格

符合殘疾稅收抵免DTC資格的人

▶申請補助金額

家庭年收入	存款金額	補助金額
低於 $ 100,392	低於 $ 500	存款金額3倍

家庭年收入	存款金額	補助金額
低於 $ 100,392	$ 500~ $ 1500	存款金額2倍
	超過 $ 1500	最高 $ 3500
超過 $ 100,392	低於 $ 1000	存款金額1倍
	超過 $ 1000	最高 $ 1000

※49歲以前存款同時可以領取補助金

※49~59歲可存款但無法領取補助金

二、免稅儲蓄帳戶 (TFSA)：

　　免稅儲蓄帳戶 (TFSA)是自2009年開始 18 歲及以上且擁有有效社會保險號碼 (SIN)的加拿大居民免稅存錢的一種方式。存款金額雖然不能作為免稅用途，但是在帳戶中賺取的收入，例如：投資收入和資本收益，通常都是免稅的。

▶申請資格

　　年滿18歲以上加拿大居民

▶存款限額

　　2022年的年度 TFSA 限額為 $ 6,000，若是當年度沒有存滿限額，則可以加到下一年度的限額，但是需特別注意僅限於下一年度為止，若是超額存款，則會有每月超額1%的罰款。例如：2021年初已經存款 $ 6,000，年底時因故提款 $ 3,000，提出來後卻反悔再存入，則2021年度會有超額 $ 3,000，每月會有1%罰款，因此建議此筆款項應等到2022年再存入。

年度	存款限額	累積存款
2022	$ 6,000	$ 81,500
2021	$ 6,000	$ 75,500
2020	$ 6,000	$ 69,500
2019	$ 6,000	$ 63,500
2018	$ 5,500	$ 57,500
2017	$ 5,500	$ 52,000
2016	$ 5,500	$ 46,500
2015	$ 10,000	$ 41,000
2014	$ 5,500	$ 31,000
2013	$ 5,500	$ 25,500
2012	$ 5,000	$ 20,000
2011	$ 5,000	$ 15,000
2010	$ 5,000	$ 10,000
2009	$ 5,000	$ 5,000

▶申請表格

➡申請免稅儲蓄帳戶TFSA需填寫表格RC240

♦ Canada Revenue Agency / Agence du revenu du Canada

Protected B when completed

Designation of an Exempt Contribution – Tax-Free Savings Account (TFSA)

Fill out this form if you are the recipient of a **survivor payment** and you wish to contribute all or a portion of it to your own TFSA, designating the contribution as an **exempt contribution**. You do not have to fill out this form if you have become the **successor holder** of the TFSA of your deceased spouse or common-law partner. This form will help you determine the maximum amount that may be designated as an exempt contribution. Call us to find out whether you can still make a designation if any of the conditions below apply to you. Many of the terms used on this form are defined on the back.

Generally, no amount of the survivor payment may be designated as an exempt contribution if any of the following applies:

- the deceased holder had an excess TFSA amount at the time of death
- payments are being received by more than one survivor
- the survivor payment or the contribution, or both, is made after the rollover period

For more information on the excess TFSA amount, or how to determine if an excess TFSA amount exists in the deceased's TFSA, go to **canada.ca/tfsa** or call **1-800-959-8281**.

Before filling out this form, you have to obtain from the executor of the estate or the TFSA issuer, the fair market value (FMV), at the time of the **holder's** death, of the TFSA from which the **survivor payment** was received. If the deceased holder had more than one TFSA, you will have to fill out a separate form to designate the contribution of each amount received, from any of the deceased holder's TFSAs, as an **exempt contribution**.

Once you have filled out Part 3 and, if required, Part 4 to determine the **maximum** amount that you can contribute and designate as an **exempt contribution**, enter the amount you want to designate in Part 5.

Send this filled out form to us within **30 days** after the date the contribution listed in Part 5 is made, or at a later time as permitted by the Minister to:

TFSA Processing Unit, Canada Revenue Agency, Sudbury Tax Centre, PO Box 20000, Station A, Sudbury ON P3A 5C1; or
TFSA Processing Unit, Canada Revenue Agency, Winnipeg Tax Centre, PO Box 14000, Station Main, Winnipeg MB R3C 3M2.

Part 1 – Survivor TFSA holder information (print)

Last name	First name and initial(s)	Social insurance number (SIN)
Address	City	Province or Territory	Postal code

Part 2 – Deceased TFSA holder information (print)

Last name	First name and initial(s)	Social insurance number (SIN)
Address	City	Province or Territory	Postal code
Name of TFSA Issuer	TFSA contract number	Date of holder's death Y Y Y Y M M D D	FMV of TFSA at time of death

Part 3 – Calculation of the amount that may be designated as an exempt contribution

Date the survivor payment was received: Year Month Day

Amount of the survivor payment received:

Total survivor payments received to date from the TFSA entered in Part 2		1
Total of any previous designations related to the payments on line 1	−	2
Line 1 **minus** line 2	=	A
FMV of the deceased holder's TFSA at the time of death from Part 2		3
Total of any previous designations related to the payments on line 1	−	4
Line 3 **minus** line 4	=	B
Enter the **lesser** amount from lines A or B		C

If the deceased holder did not have an **excess TFSA amount**, you were the only person to receive **survivor payments** from the TFSA, and the contribution is made within the **rollover period**, continue to Part 5.

However, if the deceased holder had an excess TFSA amount and you received the authorization from us to designate an amount, continue to Part 4.

Part 4 – Fill out this part when the TFSA of the deceased holder includes an excess TFSA amount

FMV of **all** deceased holder's TFSAs at date of death that ceased to be a TFSA		5
Excess TFSA amount and any related income included on line 5		6
Total of **all** previous designations related to **any** of the deceased holder's TFSAs	+	7
Line 6 **plus** line 7	= ▶ −	8
Line 5 **minus** line 8	=	D

RC240 E (21)   (Ce formulaire est disponible en français.)   Page 1 of 2

Canadä

三、商品和服務稅/統一銷售稅 (GST/HST) 抵免：

商品和服務稅/統一銷售稅 (GST/HST) 抵免是一種免稅的抵免，可幫助中低收入的個人和家庭抵消他們支付的 GST 或 HST。在加拿大幾乎所有經買賣的物品或服務都需要繳納GST。

▶**申請資格**

✓ 年滿19歲加拿大居民

✓ 有配偶或伴侶

✓ 與孩子一起生活

▶**可抵免金額**

單身

個人淨收入	沒有小孩 ($/年)	1個小孩 ($/年)	2個小孩 ($/年)	3個小孩 ($/年)	4個小孩 ($/年)
低於 $9,919	$306	$773	$934	$1,095	$1,256
$12,000	$347.62	$773	$934	$1,095	$1,256
$15,000	$407.62	$773	$934	$1,095	$1,256
$20,000	$467	$773	$934	$1,095	$1,256
$25,000	$467	$773	$934	$1,095	$1,256
$30,000	$467	$773	$934	$1,095	$1,256

個人 淨收入	沒有小孩 ($/年)	1個小孩 ($/年)	2個小孩 ($/年)	3個小孩 ($/年)	4個小孩 ($/年)
$35,000	$467	$773	$934	$1,095	$1,256
$40,000	$458.3	$764.3	$925.3	$1,086.3	$1,247.3
$45,000	$208.3	$514.3	$675.3	$836.3	$997.3
$50,000	$0	$264.3	$425.3	$586.3	$747.3
$55,000	$0	$14.3	$175.3	$336.3	$497.3
$60,000	$0	$0	$0	$86.3	$247.3
$65,000	$0	$0	$0	$0	$0

已婚

家庭 淨收入	沒有小孩 ($/年)	1個小孩 ($/年)	2個小孩 ($/年)	3個小孩 ($/年)	4個小孩 ($/年)
低於 $39,826	$612	$773	$934	$1,095	$1,256
$40,000	$603.3	$764.3	$925.3	$1,086.3	$1,247.3
$45,000	$353.3	$514.3	$675.3	$836.3	$997.3
$50,000	$103.3	$264.3	$425.3	$586.3	$747.3
$55,000	$0	$14.3	$175.3	$336.3	$497.3
$60,000	$0	$0	$0	$86.3	$247.3
$65,000	$0	$0	$0	$0	$0

▶申請表格

➡如果有孩子，申請所有兒童和家庭福利，包括 GST/HST 抵免額需填寫表格 RC66。

| ▌◆▌ Canada Revenue Agency | Agence du revenu du Canada | | **Protected B** when completed |

Canada Child Benefits Application
includes federal, provincial, and territorial programs

Find out if this form is for you

Fill out this form to apply for the Canada child benefit and register your children for the goods and services tax/harmonized sales tax (GST/HST) credit, the climate action incentive payment (CAIP) and related federal, provincial, or territorial programs the Canada Revenue Agency (CRA) administers. You can also use this form if you started a shared-custody situation for one or more children.

Do not fill out this form if you already applied using My Account on the CRA website or when you registered the birth of your newborn with your province or territory (except Yukon and Nunavut).

Who should fill out this form

The person who is **primarily responsible** for the care and upbringing of the child should apply (see "Primarily responsible for the care and upbringing of the child" on page 3).

When a child resides with a female parent in the home, the female parent is usually considered to be primarily responsible for the child and should apply. However, if the child's other parent is primarily responsible, they should apply and attach a signed letter from the female parent stating that the other parent with whom she resides is primarily responsible for all the children in the home. If the child lives with same-sex parents, only one parent should apply for all the children in the home.

For more information

For more information on the Canada child benefit, including eligibility requirements, go to **canada.ca/cra-benefits**, see Booklet T4114, Canada Child Benefit, or call 1-800-387-1193. From outside Canada or the United States, call 1-613-940-8495. We accept collect calls by automated response.

Step 1 – Your information

Social insurance number (SIN):　[| | | | | | | |]

　If you do not have a SIN, see Booklet T4114, Canada Child Benefit, under "How to apply."

First name:

Last name:

Date of birth:　[| | | | |]
　　　　　　　Year　Month　Day

Your language of correspondence:　[ ] English　[ ] Français

Phone numbers:　Home:　　　Work:　　　Ext:　　　Cell:

Step 2 – Your address

Mailing address

Apt. No. – Street No., Street name, PO Box, RR:

City:

Province or territory (or country if outside Canada):

Postal or ZIP code:

Have you moved from a different province or territory within the last 12 months?　[ ] Yes　[ ] No

　If **yes**, enter the previous province or territory and the date you moved:　　　Date: [| | | | |]
　　　　　　　　　　　　　　　　　　　　　　　　　Year　Month　Day

Home address　[ ] Same as mailing address

Apt. No. – Street No., Street name, RR:

City:

Province or territory (or country if outside Canada):

Postal or ZIP code:

RC66 E (22)　　　(Ce formulaire est disponible en français.)　　　Page 1 of 6　　　**Canada**

➡如果沒有孩子，申請個人GST/HST 抵免額需填寫表格 RC151。

▪◆▪ Canada Revenue Agency	Agence du revenu du Canada		Protected B when completed

GST/HST Credit and Climate Action Incentive Payment Application for Individuals Who Become Residents of Canada

Fill out this form to apply for the GST/HST credit, including related provincial and territorial programs, and the climate action incentive payment, for the year in which you became a resident of Canada. Use this form **only** if you don't have children. If you have children under 19 years of age, use My Account or Form RC66, Canada Child Benefits Application.

For more information, see "General information" on pages 3 and 4.

Step 1 – Your information

First name | Last name | Social insurance number

Date of birth: Year Month Day | Home telephone number | Work telephone number

Mailing address (Apt No – Street No Street name, PO Box, RR) | Your language of correspondence: ☐ English

City | Province or territory | Postal code | Votre langue de correspondance : ☐ Français

Home address, if different from mailing address (Apt No – Street No Street name, RR) | Date of address change: Year Month Day

City | Province or territory | Postal code

Marital status – Select the box that applies to your marital status on the date you **became** a resident of Canada and enter the date this marital status began (leave the date blank if you have always been single). We define each marital status on page 3.

☐ Married ☐ Living common-law ☐ Widowed ☐ Divorced ☐ Separated ☐ Single   Since Year Month Day

If your marital status has changed **since** you became a resident of Canada, select the box that applies to your new marital status and enter the date of this change:

☐ Married ☐ Living common-law ☐ Widowed ☐ Divorced ☐ Separated ☐ Single   Since Year Month Day

Step 2 – Information about your spouse or common-law partner

First name | Last name | Social insurance number

Date of birth Year Month Day | If your spouse or common-law partner's address is different than yours, enter it here; otherwise, their address will be updated to match the address indicated in Step 1.

Step 3 – Your residency status

For more information, see "Who is considered a resident of Canada" on page 3.

A – Newcomer to Canada

	You	Your spouse or common-law partner
Enter the date you, or your spouse or common-law partner, became a resident of Canada	Year Month Day	Year Month Day

B – Returning resident of Canada

	You	Your spouse or common-law partner
Enter the Canadian province or territory in which you, or your spouse or common-law partner, resided before you cut your residential ties with Canada......		
Enter the date you, or your spouse or common-law partner, cut your residential ties with Canada (became a non-resident)..	Year Month Day	Year Month Day
Enter the date you, or your spouse or common-law partner, re-established your residential ties with Canada (became a resident again)	Year Month Day	Year Month Day

RC151 E (22) | (Ce formulaire est disponible en français.) | Page 1 of 4 | Canada▪◆▪

第三節 信託

壹、何謂信託：

一、概述：

通常成立信託會簽訂一份信託合約（Trust Agreement），透過「委託人」(Settlor)、「受託人」(Trustee)及「受益人」(Beneficiaries)三個角色的連結，以更有效率而且安全的方式達到目標。

委託人於合約約定信託運作規定，將財產權移轉或為其他處分，使受託人依信託本旨，為受益人之利益或為特定之目的，管理或處分信託財產之關係。

二、成立信託的好處：

■掌控財產，降低投資風險。

■資產保護，避免繼承人理財不善。

■妥善規劃信託可以節稅。

■獨立性，信託財產與受託人固有財產相互獨立。

■信託財產不得強制執行。

■信託財產不屬於受託人的遺產。

三、成立信託的缺點：

■需要專業人士處理信託事宜，整個流程成本高。

■需要花時間處理一些文書工作。

四、信託與稅務：

稅務上每一個信託都必須申報所得稅，信託申報年度為每年1月1日至12月31日，受託人必須在年度結束後三個月內申報所得稅，提交T3報稅表。

貳、信託當事人關係：

	委託人	受託人	受益人
資格限制	無	**自然人：**律師、會計師、自己親友 **受託業者：** 1.銀行 2.證券投資信託業 3.證券投資顧問業 4.證券商	無
權利	1.保留變更/處分受益權 2.終止信託 3.選任受託人	1.請求報酬 2.信託財產留置權	1.享有及處分信託財產 2.撤銷處分
義務	移轉信託財產	信託財產管理	償還債務及支付衍生費用

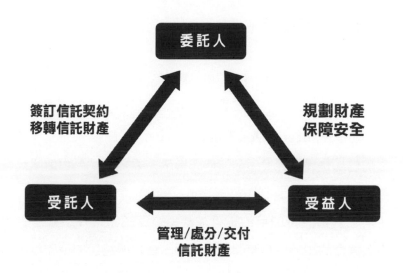

參、信託標的:

信託標的包含現金、股票、債券、商業本票、匯票等有價證券、共同基金、不動產、動產以及其他權利,例:租賃權、地上權、專利權、著作權。

信託標的特點:

■必須為積極財產,消極財產不行(債務)

■可自委託人之財產中分離

■必須現時存在

肆、信託種類:

加拿大信託類型以生前信託和遺囑信託為主。

一、生前信託(Inter Vivos Trust):

生前信託是委託人於生前的信託指示,委託人於死亡前,都可以更改信託內容。

生前信託最主要的目的是用來避免遺產認證法律手續產生之成本,遺產認證的過程時間可長可短,會根據遺產的複雜程度、受益人數量及遺囑的情況而定,一般普通認證程序需要一至兩個月,而複雜的則需要六至九個月,時間越長,費用就會越多。

生前信託一經成立即生效,原來有很多人的生前信託來分家庭收入,來減少家庭收入最高者的個人所得稅。生前信託所有的收入歸屬信託委託人,且要被徵收個人最高稅率。

二、遺囑信託(Testamentary Trust):

由遺囑建立的信託種類,此於遺囑被認證前不生任何效力。

一般遺囑信託用來保護未成年子女、配偶或同居伴侶的財產,信託成立成本較低。

於2014年2月前,遺囑信託稅率與個人稅率一樣,但遺囑信託有累進制稅率優惠，可以做為減稅的途徑之一。

於2021年2月後，累進制稅率優惠已取消，遺囑信託所有的收入都要被徵收個人最高稅率。

遺囑信託比較適合資產多的人，遺囑信託運作相對較為繁雜，所需費用也會相對比較高。

遺囑信託除了尋找專業人士應支付的服務費外，還包括下列費用：

▶遺囑檢驗費(Probate fees)：

遺囑因為需要被認證而產生遺囑檢驗費，遺囑檢驗費本質上是對遺產課徵稅金，也稱為遺囑認證稅或遺產管理稅，通常會依遺產價值而定，遺囑檢驗費通常由省政府徵收。

加拿大各省遺囑檢驗費如下：

省份	遺產價值達100萬加幣	遺產價值達200萬加幣
BC省	13,650加幣	27,650加幣
AB省	525加幣	525加幣
SK省	7,000加幣	14,000加幣
MB省	X	X
ON省	14,250加幣	29,250加幣

省份	遺產價值達100萬加幣	遺產價值達200萬加幣
魁北克省	X	X
NB省	5,000加幣	10,000加幣
NS省	16,258加幣	33,208加幣
PEI省	4,000加幣	8,000加幣
NL省	6,054加幣	12,054加幣
育空地區	140加幣	140加幣
西北地區	435加幣	435加幣
努納武特	400加幣	400加幣

除了遺囑外，另一個為財務授權書(Financial Powers of Attorney)是生前的意外財務安排，當遇上意外或健康狀況不佳，以致無法親自處理日常生活財務時，財務授權書有如遺囑，授權他人於授權範圍內進行財產之必要運作。

遺囑是相當重要的文件，在BC省如果去世後沒有留有遺囑，遺產會依照遺產管理法案(Wills, Estate and Successions Act)所列的方式來處理。

遺囑可以依照自己的意思將遺產分給所選擇之繼承人，亦可減少稅務負擔。在準備遺囑時，建議與專業人士做討論，以免日後在稅務或分配上有問題。

三、自益信託：為自己利益所設立之信託，委託人及受益人為自
　　己。

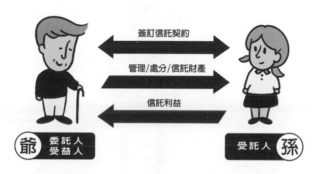

四、他益信託：為他人利益所設立之信託，委託人及受益人非同
　　一人。

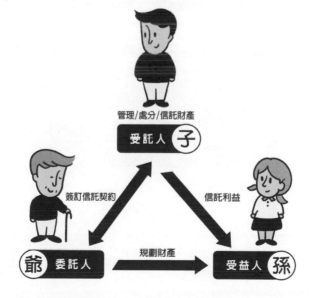

五、部分自益部分他益：為自己及他人利益所設立之信託，受益
人為自己及他人。

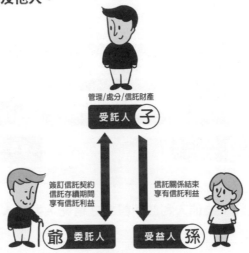

六、不特定或尚未存在的信託：為他人利益所設立之信託，受益
人為不特定或尚未存在。

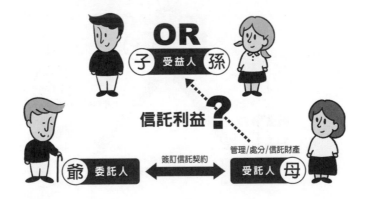

七、公益信託：為公共利益、增進社會福祉所設立，以慈善、文化、學術、技藝、宗教、祭祀或其他公眾利益目的之信託。

伍、成立信託：

一、成立信託前置作業：

1.金融專業人士或律師：

信託案件如果較為複雜，建議找專業人士指導降低信託無效的風險，但相對來說費用成本高。

2.受僱公司：有些公司曾提供員工遺產規劃服務。

3.自行處理：費用成本低，需要付出時間做功課。

二、準備信託合約：

信託合約應包括以下內容：

■確認委托人、受託人及受益人

■信託標的

■信託運作方式，如：移轉信託財產時間

■原受託人無法執行信託財產管理，如何選任繼任受託人。

■可準備信託證書留存於處理信託之專業人士。

三、簽署信託合約：

信託當事人確認信託合約內容無誤後簽署，並建議進行合約公證，以確保簽署之有效性。

四、開立信託銀行帳戶：

信託合約簽署後可開立一個信託銀行帳戶，專門存放信託資產。

五、委託人交付信託標的

委託人需移轉信託標的予受託人。

六、受託人依信託合約執行信託計劃

受託人需依簽署之信託合約內容管理或處分信託財產。

第四章

加拿大
公司稅務

第一節 公司設立

壹、公司組織型態：

加拿大常見的公司型態有獨資公司、合夥公司及有限公司，其中又以有限公司最為常見，以下分別就這三種公司型態作介紹。

一、Sole Proprietorship獨資公司：

以個人名義設立的公司，由個人一人出資及負責公司營運，與台灣獨資企業類似。優點是個人擁有100%公司所有權，並享有公司全部的獲利，且公司每年稅務可以與個人稅務一同申報，程序上較為簡化；但缺點就是個人須承擔無限責任，即如果公司產生債務必須由個人承擔所有虧損。

二、Partnership合夥公司：

由兩個或兩個以上的個人或法人共同出資經營的公司，類似台灣合夥創業，合夥人不一定需以金錢方式出資。

合夥公司又可以分為

■**普通合夥：** 兩個或兩個以上的「個人」所組成，合夥人共同享有公司獲利，決議方式必須所有合夥人同意，且對於公司債務每個合夥人都要承擔所有虧損。

■**有限合夥：**一個或多個「無限責任」合夥人和「有限責任」合夥人組成，「有限責任」合夥人僅就出資額承擔有限責任，類似台灣的兩合公司。

■**有限責任合夥Limited Liability Partnership(LLP)：**由一個股東負責公司所有營運及債務處理，其餘股東則為「有限投資人(Limited Partner)」承擔責任以出資額為限，但無權參與公司運作，有限責任合夥同時有「股份有限公司」的有限責任特徵，也包含「合夥」的直接管理權特徵。

三、Incorproated有限公司：

由兩個以上股東出資組成，每位股東僅就出資額承擔公司的債務，通常以「Ltd」、「Inc.」、「Corp.」結尾。優點是穩定經營，公司設立後不會因為股東變動或離職等原因而關閉；在稅務方面優惠也比較多，公司營業額在50萬加幣以下的中小企業，能享有各種稅務優惠，詳細稅務介紹在後面章節會說明；有限公司缺點就是雜費支出會比較多，例如：水電費、郵電費、辦公室用品購置等都屬於雜費支出，且有限公司需要獨立報稅，不得與負責人個人稅務一起申報。

對於來加拿大做生意，一般建議以成立「有限公司」來營運，主要原因就是股東只需承擔「有限債務」(Limited liability)。

貳、公司設立：

加拿大設立公司有聯邦法規以及省的法規，兩者規範各有所不同，依聯邦法規設立的公司為「聯邦公司」，依省的法規設立的公司為「省公司」，以下會就兩者做說明。

一、聯邦公司 V.S. 省公司：

在加拿大設立公司並非所有人都可以自由選擇要設立聯邦公司或省公司；如為加拿大公民，在加拿大成立公司可以選擇依《加拿大商業公司法》(Canada Business Corporation Act-CBCA)成立「聯邦公司」或依《省公司法》成立「省公司」；而非加拿大公民則只能依《加拿大商業公司法》成立「聯邦公司」；而唯獨BC省對於非加拿大公民設立公司限制最為寬鬆，並不要求公司董事一定要是加拿大公民。

《省公司法》由各省制定，例如：在安大略省(ON省)就是《安省商業公司法》(Business Corporation Act-OBCA)；在魁北克省(QC省)就是《魁省公司法》(Companies Act-QCA)。

　　無論是「聯邦公司」或「省公司」都必須有一個公司名稱，公司名稱必須通過加拿大「公司名稱檢索系統」預查並取得檢索報告書，這概念與在台灣設立公司要預查是類似的流程；而聯邦公司名稱查詢範圍是全加拿大，省公司則以該省為查詢範圍。

　　「聯邦公司」優點為核准設立後得以同一公司名稱在加拿大各省經營，而「省公司」如要跨省經營，必須做跨省登記及公司名註冊；但聯邦公司相較於省公司來說，設立費用及程序上比較昂貴及繁瑣。

二、設立流程：

1.選定公司名稱：

　　無論為「聯邦公司」或「省公司」都必須選定擬用之公司名稱，須向聯邦政府或省政府相關主管機關申請核定，此申請會收取規費，為避免選擇的公司名稱不能使用，可以提供多個名稱做選擇。

　　一般公司名稱可以使用英文字或數字，而外國公司在加拿大設立分公司，需要在名稱中加上「加拿大」，與其母公司作區別。

2.選定設立地址：

　　選定之地址必須真實存在，自家住所也可以做為營業地；設立聯邦公司營業地點包括整個加拿大，但需注意的是，設立省公司，其營業地點必須在該省範圍內，如果在其他省份設立營業地點或分支機構，必須在該省另行辦理設立手續。

3.資本額(Capital)：加拿大不要求最低資本額。

4.營業項目及營業方式：

公司營業項目基本上除毒品、槍械、電視廣播業、金融業、新聞出版業、航空業等特許行業外，一般不做限制；營業方式也不限制。

5.編制公司章程(Bylaw)：

制定公司章程，內容必須包括公司名稱、股本、股份移轉限制、董事人數、營業項目、營運方式、股東、董事等公司成員之權利義務，且記載事項不得與聯邦加拿大商業公司法或省公司法相抵觸；公司章程訂定後，須經公司每位創辦成員確認並簽署。

6.公司成員：

股東(Shareholder)：至少一名，自然人或法人皆可擔任，國籍不受限制；但若為外國人在加拿大設立公司，公司股東要有一定比例為加拿大公民，例如：聯邦公司股東中要有至少25%的加拿大公民或永久居民作為董事會成員；省公司各省有所不同，一般要求50%的加拿大公民或永久居民為股東。

■**董事(Director)：**至少一名，必須為18歲以上之自然人，國籍不受限制。

■**職員(Officer)：**不一定為股東，通常會設有總裁(President)及秘書(Secretary)。

7.銀行開戶：

公司設立後要在銀行開立企業帳戶，不得與個人銀行帳戶混用。

 # 第二節 加拿大公司營運

壹、公司營運文件：

加拿大從設立公司到公司營運，必須取得兩份文件：公司登記證書及營業執照。

一、公司登記證書：

公司設立完成後會取得公司登記證書，「聯邦公司」由聯邦政府發出；「省公司」由省政府發出。

二、營業執照(Business License)：

營業執照由市政府發出，效期為一年，需每年更換一次，沒有營業執照的公司不得刻公司印鑑章、簽合約、註冊商標、刊登廣告及銀行開戶。

如果公司同時經營多個不同性質的營業項目，市政府會要求營業人申請不止一份營業執照，也會有其他條件要求，例如：零售店及餐廳必須在零售業區域內營業，工業要在工業區域內營運，以住家作為公司營業處所不得僱用家庭成員工作等。

貳、聘僱勞工規範：

聯邦政府及各省政府均有各自聘僱勞工之規範，本書以聯邦政府及BC省為例，主要依據法令為聯邦加拿大勞動法(Canada Labour Code) 及BC省僱傭標準法例(Employment Standards Act)。

一、工資：

聯邦規定的最低工資為15.55加幣/時；BC省最低工資目前為
15.20加幣/時，一般勞工每月最少可以領取兩次薪資，雇主必須
於計算薪資後8日內，支付。無論是聯邦法或BC省政府法令均有
規定支付勞工薪資須扣除加拿大退休金(CPP)、就業保險金(EI)及
所得稅。

二、工作時間：

每日工作時間不超過8小時，每週工作時間不超過40小時，每
週有一日為休息日，連續工作達5小時應有30分鐘用餐時間；如
果工作超過法定工作時間，雇主應給付加班費；如為輪班制應給
予至少連續8小時的休息時間。

聯邦政府有特別規範下列職業之勞工不適用前述工作時間：

■卡車司機
■西海岸、東海岸及五大湖船舶航運業
■鐵路營運人員
■廣播業銷售人員
■銀行業銷售人員

三、加班費及加班時數：

1.每日計算：

■超過8小時雇主應支付1.5倍工資。

■超過12小時雇主應支付2倍工資。

例：

	Mon	Tue	Wed	Thu	Fri
正常時數	8	8	8	8	0
1.5倍	0	2	0	4	0
2倍	0	0	0	1	0
總時數	8	10	8	13	0

一週工作總時數：39

支付1.5倍薪資時數：6

支付2倍薪資時數：1

2.每週計算：

每週平均最長工作時數為48小時，有特殊情況者除外。

■超過40小時雇主應支付1.5倍工資。

■超過48小時雇主應支付2倍工資。

例：

	Mon	Tue	Wed	Thu	Fri	Sat
正常時數	8	8	8	8	8	5
1.5倍	0	0	0	0	0	0
2倍	0	0	0	0	0	0
總時數	8	8	8	8	8	5

一週工作總時數：45

支付1.5倍薪資時數：5

3. 平均工時協議書(Averaging Agreement)：

勞資雙方可簽署協議書，每週工作40小時，可分散在2~4週。

例：

週一至週四工作10小時，週五休息，一週工作40小時。

四、休假及國定假日：

1. 特休：

工作滿1年可以享有14天特休(年假)。

工作滿5年可以享有21天特休(年假)。

2.假期薪資：

勞工可以選擇領取假期薪資取代特休：

工作滿1年可以享有薪資1年總收入4%。

工作滿5年可以享有薪資1年總收入6%。

假期薪資應於每年度特休開始前7日支付。

3.法定假日(公眾假期)：

勞工於受雇後30日內工作15日可以享受有薪的法定假日(公眾假期)。

4.法定假別：

加拿大法定假別可分為有薪假及無薪假：

■**無薪假：**病假、工傷病假、產假、育嬰假、照護假、重大疾病假、兒童死亡或失蹤假、傳統習俗假、開庭或陪審團假、COVID-19確診假、入伍假

■**有薪假：**喪假(支付3日)、事假(支付3日)、家暴受害者假(支付5日)

五、終止勞動關係：

1.勞工自願離職：無須提前通知雇主。

2.雇主終止勞動關係須提前預告：

已工作3個月以上12個月以下：1週前書面通知解聘或支付1週資遣費。

已工作12個月以上3年以下：2週前書面通知解聘或支付2週資遣費。

已工作3年以上：每年增加一週書面通知解聘或支付資遣費。

3.雇主終止勞動關係無須提前預告：

如雇主有充分理由認定勞工有違反公司規則或違法行為者，無須預告通知或支付資遣費，就可以直接解聘勞工。

 # 第三節 公司稅務

壹、商業編號
(Business Account Number)：

營業人必須向加拿大稅務局(CRA)申請商業編號，才能進行後續聯邦、省及市政府稅務申報事宜，應申請的商業編號包含：

■GST/HST商品及服務稅編號：營業人在加拿大境內販售應稅商品及服務，且年營業額在30,000加幣以上者須申請。

■Payroll Deductions薪資扣繳編號：營業人依規定要扣繳員工個人所得稅(Income Tax)、養老保險金(CPP)及就業保險金(EI)等須申請。

■Corporation Income Tax公司所得稅編號：公司申報所得稅須申請。

■Import-Export進出口編號：將貨品進口到加拿大或出口到其他國家須申請。

WSIB勞工賠償委員會編號：營業人有僱用員工且支薪，應依核定費率繳納保費須申請。

貳、公司稅務種類：

加拿大公司稅務種類繁多，包含GST、HST、PST、公司所得稅、薪資扣繳等，以下分別介紹詳細內容。

一、GST (Goods & Services Tax)商品及服務稅：

又稱貨勞稅，即貨物增值稅(Value-added tax)，加拿大聯邦政府於1991年開始實施，目前稅率為5%。在加拿大消費標示金額通常是「未稅價」，所以結帳時會加上GST，一般由消費者負擔，營業人負責申報。

營業人除了小型供應商(Small Suppliers)、免稅商品或服務(Exempt Supplies)外，都必須向聯邦政府申報GST。

小型供應商(Small Suppliers)可自由選擇是否申報GST，如選擇申報，應向消費者收取GST，並向政府申請退還代墊之GST；如選擇申報，則不能向消費者收取GST，也不可向政府申請退還代墊之GST。申報GST的時間會依公司年營業額而有所不同：

每年營業額(加幣)	申報期限
1,500,000元以下	每年一次
1,500,000~6,000,000元	每三個月一次(每季)
6,000,000元以上	每月一次

免稅商品或服務(Exempt Supplies)包含：

■長期住宅或租屋　　　　　■舊屋買賣

■有執照的牙醫治療　　　　■托兒服務

■教育部准許的教育課程　　■國內渡輪服務

■法律援助服務　　　　　　■金融及保險服務

零稅率商品或服務(Zero-rated supplies)包含：

■基本糧食(如：牛奶、麵包、蔬菜)

■穀物、毛皮、乾菸草等農產品

■農場牲畜

■漁業產品

■出口貨品

■醫療處方藥品及醫療器具

■女性衛生用品

加拿大有些省份或地區僅徵收GST：

	GST	PST
AB省	5%	X
努納武特	5%	X
西北地區	5%	X
育空地區	5%	X

AB省特殊應稅項目有：

■住宿稅：4%

■酒店住房稅：4%

二、HST (Harmonized Sales Tax)合併銷售稅：

1997年4月1日由加拿大聯邦政府推出，將商品及服務稅(GST)和省稅(PST)結合，向大部份商品買賣及服務供應商徵收合併銷售稅(HST)，稅率會因各省省稅而有所不同。

目前只有ON省、NB省、NS省、NL省及PEI省徵收合併銷售稅(HST)，通常由加拿大稅務局(CRA)收取後，再將稅金分發給上述省份。

ON省、NB省、NS省、NL省徵收合併銷售稅(HST)之稅率：

	GST	PST	HST
ON省	5%	8%	13%
NB省	5%	10%	15%
NS省	5%	10%	15%
NL省	5%	10%	15%
PEI省	5%	10%	15%

ON省銷售稅一般稅率為8%，不同商品或服務有不同的稅率：

■企業添購物品及辦公室設備、電腦、影印機等：8%

■販售熟食單價4加幣以上：8%

■製造業廠商添購機器設備：0%

■旅館住宿業設立未滿一個月：5%

■娛樂場所門票單價4加幣以上：10%

■餐廳銷售含酒精飲料：10%

■零售含酒精飲料12%

三、PST省稅：

省級的銷售稅，稅率會因省而異，且不同商品或服務有不同的稅率。

	GST	PST	GST/PST
BC省	5%	7%	**12%**
MB省	5%	7%	**12%**
QC省	5%	9.975%	**14.975%**
SK省	5%	6%	**11%**

1. BC省銷售稅(B.C. Sales Tax)：

聯邦政府推出的合併銷售稅(HST)於2010年7月1日實施後，遭BC省市民全民公投否決，致BC省政府於2013年3月31日取消徵收合併銷售稅(HST)，改以實施B.C.省銷售稅制度(GST/PST)。

B.C.省銷售稅一般稅率為7%，也有特殊稅率：

■含酒精飲料：10%

■溫哥華市中心停車費：24%

■買汽車：

車價(加幣)	稅率
55,000元以下	7%
55,000~55,999元	8%
56,000~56,999元	9%
57,000~124,999元	10%
125,000~149,999元	15%
150,000元以上	20%

B.C.省銷售稅特殊應稅項目有：

■酒精飲料、大麻產品、蘇打飲料(2021年4月1日起)

■汽車(含租賃服務)

■建築材料、家用或辦公家具

■租賃服務、維修保養服務、軟體服務、法律服務、電信服務、
住宿服務

B.C.省銷售稅無須應稅項目有：

■童裝

■包裝服務、房地產買賣服務、室內設計服務、會計服務

■交通運輸服務、拖車服務、驗車服務、洗車服務

■洗衣服務、美容美髮服務、牙科、舞蹈教學

■批發商

■小型供應商(small seller)-每年營業額低於1萬加幣

如何徵收B.C.省銷售稅：

營業人每月將應徵收的銷售稅額寄給B.C.省政府，如同時經營應稅項目與無須應稅項目，營業人要將兩個項目分別列出，在應稅項目加上7% B.C.省銷售稅。

B.C.省銷售稅對營業人的影響：

對應稅之營業人來說，與營業相關所購買之貨品，無須負擔銷售稅；但其他與營業不相關所購買之貨品，如機器、電腦、文具等，營業人必須負擔銷售稅，及提高營業人經營成本。

2.MB省銷售稅：

特殊應稅項目有：

■住宿稅：5%

■酒店住房稅：5%

3. QC省銷售稅：

特殊應稅項目有：

■書籍：5%

■旅遊住宿：3.5%

4. SK省銷售稅：

自2017年4月1日起，新房屋、餐廳、加熱食品和飲料均需繳納PST，而酒類產品為特殊稅率10%。

四、Income tax所得稅：

公司所得稅詳細申報內容可參考本章第四節。

(一)公司所得稅類別：

依公司持有財產的動機及員工參與程度分為營利所得與財產所得：

■營利所得：屬於維持公司日常營運。

■財產所得：屬於長期投資，如財產出租所得、財產出售所得。

(二)聯邦所得稅：

一般聯邦稅率為38%，而公司在加拿大各省的收入得依《企業所得稅法》享受10%聯邦稅收減免即適用28%稅率，但若為加拿大境外收入不適用聯邦稅收減免。

公司符合條件者可享有13%聯邦稅收減免即適用15%稅率，但下列情形不適用：

1.符合小型企業扣除標準和加拿大製造和加工所得。

2.可抵扣生產銷售電能產品或生產銷售蒸汽產品之所得。

3.符合可退稅規定的投資收益。

4.個人服務業、投資公司、抵押貸款投資公司、共有基金公司取得的收入。

如為加拿大控股私人公司(CCPC)所得為50萬加幣適用9%稅率。

如為小型企業所得為50萬加幣適用19%稅率。

(三)省所得稅：

每個省所得稅稅率可分為較低稅率和較高稅率：

■較低稅率：適用於所得為50~60萬加幣的聯邦小型企業。

■較高稅率：適用於其他公司。

■各省稅率表：

省份	較高稅率	較低稅率	所得限額
NL省	15%	3%	50萬加幣
NS省	14%	2.5%	50萬加幣
NB省	14%	2.5%	50萬加幣
PEI省	16%	1%	50萬加幣
ON省	11.5%	3.2%	50萬加幣
MB省	12%	0%	50萬加幣
SK省	12%	0%	60萬加幣
BC省	12%	2%	50萬加幣
努納福特	12%	3%	50萬加幣
NT地區	11.5%	2%	50萬加幣
YK地區	12%	0%	50萬加幣

五、Import-export tax聯邦進出口稅：

加拿大海關對進口貨物徵收的進口關稅。自1988年起加拿大採用協調制度(Harmonized Commodity Description and Coding System-HS)，除免稅之貨品外，所有商業性進口均須繳納關稅和銷售稅，課徵標準依產地不同、貨物的性質或其價值而有所差別，如佣金、經紀費、包裝費、特許權使用費和運費，以下為進口非應稅進口商品：

■在加拿大0%稅率之商品。

■在加拿大境外比賽中獲得的獎牌、獎杯和其他獎品。

■政府或指定機構免費進口之旅遊文獻。

■慈善機構進口且捐贈給慈善單位的商品。

■因維護或修理目的而進口之貨物，且貨物在加拿大境內期間所有權或使用人未變更，並於貨物完成服務後立即出口。

■製造業公司進口並有進口證書，經加拿大境外公司加工後出口，且未在加拿大境內使用的商品。

■由外國人或境外公司提供免費更換貨物、零件。

■透過郵寄或快遞寄往加拿大境內之20加幣以下商品，但以下商品除外：

1.啤酒、菸草和葡萄酒。

2.書籍、報紙、雜誌、期刊和類似出版物。

3.從加拿大零售商購買並從加拿大境外郵寄的商品。

出口的部分則無須課徵銷售稅。無論進口或出口之商品及服務均包含無形資產。

營業人透過「出口配送中心計劃」和「加工服務出口商計劃」，可以獲得進出口稅的減免資格。

■Export Distribution Centre Program出口配送中心計劃 (EDCP)：

EDCP效期為三年，該計劃允許有附加價值之出口導向型企業，只做商品的加工或配送，為商品增加有限的附加價值，但不進行製造或生產，無需繳納稅金。

獲得EDCP 資格必須專門從事商業活動，出口收入達90%以上，不會對財產為重大處分，為商品總增值在20%以下。

■Exporters of Processing Services Program加工服務出口商計劃(EOPS)：

EOPS效期也是三年，該計劃僅限於在加拿大加工、存放或銷售而進口貨品，且必須未在加拿大境內消費或使用的情況下出口。這裡所謂的「加工」包括調整、修改、組裝、組合、合併、拆卸、清潔、維護、修理、檢查、測試、包裝。

EOPS資格必須與進口貨品的境外廠商沒有商業上密切往來關係，且在加拿大不會進口貨品或出口加工產品，也不會將進口貨品或加工產品移轉給他人，最後一點，進口貨品必須在四年內出口。

六、Payroll Deductions聯邦薪資扣繳：

雇主支付員工薪資應扣減下列項費用，並按時向加拿大稅務局(CRA)繳納：

■加拿大退休金(Canada Pension Plan)

■就業保險金(Employment Insurance)

■所得稅(Income Tax)

(一)加拿大退休金Canada Pension Plan(CPP)：

1.一般勞工：

加拿大退休金是提供加拿大勞工退休養老的一個保障，為每月應稅福利，在退休時可領取的收入，通常由雇主代為繳納，類似台灣的勞保。

一般18~65歲的勞工都可以享有領取退休金的資格，而65~70歲的勞工則可選擇是否參與CPP退休金制度。退休金繳納超過一年就可以享有退休後領取退休金的資格，一般是在65歲申請提領，依規定60歲就可以開始提領，最晚70歲前提領完畢。

雇主於支付員工薪資時應扣除退休金，公司本身亦必須負擔相同金額之退休金(CPP)，連同就業保險金(EI)和所得稅(Income Tax)一併繳納給政府。

2.雇主本身與自僱者：

　　自僱者(Self-Employed)一般由自己負擔退休金；雇主即公司負責人如有領薪資，必須自己從薪資中扣除退休金繳納，公司本身亦必須負擔相同金額之退休金(CPP)。

3.計算方式：

　　計算公式：(每月薪資-每月基本扣除額)xCPP費率

　　2022年度基本扣除額：3,500加幣

　　每月基本扣除額：3,500/12=291.67加幣

　　CPP費率：5.7%

　　2022年最高薪資限額：64,900加幣

　　2022年CPP最高給付額：(64,900-3,500)x5.7%=3,499.8加幣

　　案例：

　　A員工2022年每月薪資：5,000加幣

　　每月CPP計算：(5,000-291.67)x5.7%=**268.37加幣**

　　員工負擔部分：268.37加幣

　　公司負擔部分：268.37加幣

　　總計每月應繳納政府的CPP：268.37+268.37=**536.74加幣**

(二)就業保險金Employment Insurance(EI)：

1.一般勞工：

　　加拿大的失業勞工可以享有聯邦政府就業保險金(EI)福利，這項福利是由加拿大就業和社會發展部(ESDC)管理。

　　加拿大大多數雇主都會為其員工投保就業保險金，雇主和員工都要負擔，通常由雇主代為繳納，且雇主還需另外負擔1.4倍的就業保險金。

　　雇主應於員工離職時，交付員工就業紀錄Record of Employment(ROE)，讓員工可以申請就業保險金。

2.雇主本身及自僱者：

　　自僱者已成為加拿大公民者，可以在參與自僱人士計劃後12個月內享有此EI福利；而雇主即公司負責人持有40%以上公司股份者，則無法享有EI福利。

3.計算方式：

　　計算公式：每月薪資 x EI費率

　　2022年就業保險金費率：1.58%

　　2022年最高投保薪資限額：60,300加幣

　　2022年EI最高給付限額：60,300 x 1.58%=952.74加幣

　　案例：

A員工每月薪資：5,000加幣

每月EI計算：5,000 x 1.58%=**79加幣**

員工負擔部分：79加幣

雇主另外負擔1.4倍：79 x 1.4=110.6加幣

雇主負擔部分：79+110.6=189.6加幣

總計每月應繳納政府的EI：79+79+110.6=**268.6加幣**

(三)個人所得稅Income Tax：

雇主支付員工薪資，必須從中扣除所得稅(Income Tax)，個人所得稅內容可詳閱前面章節。

(四)Payroll Deductions薪資扣繳運作：

綜上，雇主於支付員工薪資時應扣除退休金(CPP)、就業保險金(EI)和個人所得稅(Income Tax)後，代為員工繳納給政府。

自1995年起加拿大稅務局提供免費軟體，在計算加拿大退休金(CPP)、就業保險金(EI)及個人所得稅(Income Tax)更加便利、快速及準確。

案例：

A員工2022年每月薪資：5,000加幣

加拿大退休金(CPP)：**268.37加幣**

就業保險金(EI)：**79加幣**

個人所得稅：**500加幣**

員工每月實領薪資：5,000-268.37-79-500=4,142.63加幣

每月應繳納政府金額：(268.37+268.37)+(79+79+110.6)+500

=1,305.34加幣

薪資扣繳政府也訂有繳納期限如下，未按時繳納者，加拿大稅務局會追加利息及罰款，情況嚴重者恐有刑事責任：

每月應繳納金額低於25,000加幣	次月15日前繳納
每月平均應繳納金額為 25,000~99,999.99加幣＋ 支付薪資：每月1~15日	當月25日前繳納
支付薪資：每月16日至月底	次月10日前繳納
每月平均應繳納金額為100,000加幣以上＋ 支付薪資：分四期支付(1-7日/8-14日/15-21日/22日-月底)	每期末3日內繳納
每月應繳納金額低於3,000加幣＋ 過去12個月內均於期限內繳納	雇主可申請改為每季繳納

七、Workers' Compensation勞工賠償：

勞工因工作受傷、生病甚至是死亡，所謂勞工包括在加拿大境外工作的員工，均可依加拿大勞工賠償法案(Workers' Compensation Act)請求賠償，這些賠償包括收入損失補償、醫療相關服務、復健服務以及其家屬可獲得撫卹金，員工因此所獲得的工傷賠償無須算進收入繳納所得稅。

勞工賠償為不可追究責任制度，即如已取得勞工賠償，不得再對雇主採取法律行動。

目前勞工賠償是由各省勞工賠償委員會Workers' Compensation Board(WCB)來管理及執行賠償事宜，賠償費用將依行業別和員工薪資來估算。

■以B.C.省為例-WorkSafe BC：

不論是全職、兼職、約聘勞工或打工者，甚至是公司負責人均受到WorkSafe BC的保護。

保護範圍：因工受傷、因工患病導致殘疾、甚至死亡

因工受傷：勞工在工作時受傷，或者傷勢是由工作造成。

勞工賠償流程：

雇主得知員工因工受傷或患病後3日內向WorkSafeBC報告

WorkSafeBC收到後會建立索賠申請

如雇主未進行勞工賠償：

1.主管機關將會進行罰款。

2.如員工因工受傷且提出申訴，由雇主負擔全部賠償費用。

3.雇主應補繳納勞工保險費用。

4.雇主因工受傷無法獲得賠償。

參、報稅期間：

加拿大一般會計年度為4月1日至3月31日，而各項稅務必須自會計年度最後一日起6個月內申報完成。

 # 第四節 公司所得稅申報

壹、營業收入：

公司應納稅額以營業收入計算之，營業收入包含投資、經營、財產轉讓和其他營業活動中取得收入金額，包括銷售商品或是提供勞務等所收到的錢，每一筆收入必須有原始憑證，如：發票、收據及合約等）來佐證記錄中所有收入。

一、應納稅收入：

1.股息紅利：

一般公司獲得之股息紅利應計入營業收入，如公司已向股東分配股利，先前已繳納之所得稅可向稅務局申請退還。

2.資本獲利：

資本獲利金額之50%減去資本虧損後之餘額，應計入公司營業收入中。

3.一般租金收入

4.農業或商業運營土地的租賃收益

5.準備金：

支付未來費用或賠償而預留的資金。

6.政府補助

二、減免及抵扣所得稅：

1.來自加拿大應稅公司之股息紅利：可以全額抵扣所得稅。

2.其他可減免所得稅之企業：

減免企業	減免內容	資格要求
學徒制企業	1.可減免學徒薪資10%。 2.最高減免限額2,000加幣	1.經政府認證的學徒制公司。 2.屬於加拿大指定技術行業管理協會(Red Seal Trades)列舉的技術職業。 3.技術職業有取得證照
電影影片製作	1.可減免勞力成本25%。 2.最高減免額度不得超過製作成本總額15%。	1.適用於加拿大應稅公司。 2.公司需繳納製作成本總額0.3%的申請費(不得低於200加幣)。 3.已符合電影/錄像制作服務稅收抵免的企業,不適用該政策。
電影影片製作服務	1.可減免加拿大國民薪資總額16%。 2.沒有最高減免額度限制。	1.適用於加拿大私人公司和在加拿大常設機構(非私人公司) 2.公司需繳納5,000加幣申請費。
科學研究與實驗開發	1.在加拿大從事工業研究與開發,可減免研究開發費35%。 2.研究開發費包括薪資、研發材料、機器設備、實驗開發、應用研究、基礎科學研究和特定類型技術工作之費用。	無

三、免課徵所得稅的企業：

1.特定販售房屋公司：

專門為老年人提供低價房屋，且公司收入不分配給雇主、員工及股東的公司。

2.特定組織機構：

公司收入不分配給雇主、員工及股東之農業機構、貿易委員會、商會等。

3.互助保險公司(Mutual Insurance Corporations)：

公司保險費收入全部來自教堂、學校和其他慈善機構等。

4.養老金信託公司：

管理養老金計劃的信託公司。

5.小型投資企業：

按相關法令規定成立的小型投資企業。

6.從事科學研究和實驗發展的「非營利」企業：

從事或促進科學研究和實驗發展，且公司收入不分配給雇主、員工及股東，並在納稅期間滿足下列要求：

■未從事生產經營。

■在加拿大每一筆花費用於科學研究和實驗發展。

貳、費用：

只要是公司營運的花費、非私人費用以及加拿大稅法中特別列出的項目都可以做為公司費用，從收入中扣減費用需保留費用的原始憑證。

公司營運實際發生的營業支出即費用，除加拿大稅法另有規定外，可以抵扣所得稅。可抵扣之費用不必與具體項目收入有直接關聯或產生經濟利益，也無須一定要在當年度就實現收入。

一、可抵扣所得稅之費用：

1.設立公司費用：

設立公司費用在3,000加幣以下可全額作費用從收入中扣除；3,000加幣以上費用將算入折舊，每年以5%折舊率遞減。

2.餐飲和娛樂費用：

■50%的餐飲娛樂費用可以從收入中扣除。

■公司員工聚餐或設立慈善機構舉行聚餐可以100%扣除。

■主要營業收入為餐飲、娛樂服務的公司，可扣除營業相關之費用。

■經加拿大國家稅務局(CRA)認定具有公益捐贈資格的公益性社會團體籌款活動的支出。

3.廣告費用：

包括報紙、電視台和廣播電台的廣告費用。

4.執照費及會費：

包括營業執照、汽機車牌照或協會會費等。

5.保險費用：

公司營運之房屋、機器設備等商業保險費用。

6.利息及銀行手續費

7.修繕及維護費用：

公司擁有之財產維修費用。

8.辦公室用品費用：

包含文具、文件櫃、辦公室桌椅等。

9.會計及法律服務費用：

會計及法律專業服務和諮詢費用。

例如：納稅義務人有與營運相關的應收帳款，為收取應收帳款而產生之法律服務費用就可以做抵扣。

10.員工薪資

11.融資費用：

融資費用可以在五年內做抵扣，可抵扣20%，納稅年度不足12個月者，可按比例抵扣。

融資費用一般包括以下內容：

1.證券交易之傭金和費用。

2.因公開募股產生的法律服務費用。

3.因借款或公開募股產生的會計或審計費用。

4.公開募股說明書或股票相關的印製費用。

5.與融資相關的承諾或擔保支出。

6.可抵扣之損失(營業損失或與營運相關之擔保損失)。

例如:製造業者為了確保將來原物料正常供應,維持公司正常營運,會為此原物料之供應商擔保債務,因此做擔保之相關費用可以抵扣。

12.資本性支出(Capital expenditures):

一般資本性支出不能用來抵稅,但可做為折舊扣除,折舊計算採餘額遞減法,例:

■汽車:折舊率30%

■家具及設備:折舊率20%

■影印機及電子通訊設備:折舊率20%

■電腦應用軟體:折舊率100%

■桌上型電腦、平板電腦、存儲設備、螢幕、磁碟機、電纜、影印機及其系統軟體:折舊率55%

■用於製造和加工的機器設備:折舊率30%(1992年後取得)

■設立公司費用(3000加幣以上):可抵稅限額3000加幣,剩

餘金額折舊率5%

■房屋：

→折舊率4%(1987年後取得)

→折舊率10%(2007年3月18日後取得且用於製造和加工)

→折舊率6%(非居住用之房屋)

■土地：不能折舊

■採礦設備及挖掘設備(1987年後取得)：折舊率30%

■模具、夾具和模型：折舊率100%

■公司股票：不能折舊

資本性支出需要特別留意，做會計記帳時應將資本性支出分開列出。

有些資產折舊採直線法，例：

■租賃資產改良之支出：以租賃有效期限加續租一年，作為攤銷年限進行分攤，最低攤銷年限為五年。

二、不可抵扣所得稅之費用：

1.不合理的費用支出。

2.所得稅法未規定准予扣除的資本性支出。

3.所得稅法規定准予因免徵所得稅之收入所產生之費用支出。

4.準備金支出：除經稅務機關認定可抵扣外，通常不可做抵扣。

5.罰款與罰金：

　　2004年3月22日以後發生之罰款不得抵扣，且此規定亦適用於違反外國法律產生之罰款。然2004年3月22日之前發生的罰款，是因公司營運所造成者可以抵扣，但嚴重違反國家政策者除外，例如：因向加拿大政府官員、司法人員非法行賄之罰款。

參、應納稅額計算：

一、計算方法：

　　納稅義務人應依利潤表計算該納稅年度之淨所得，接著扣除特定扣除項，就可得出應納稅所得額。應納稅所得額確定後乘以所得稅率計算就可計算出應付所得稅金。納稅義務人可將可抵扣所得稅金之項目在應付稅金中扣除，扣除後之金額即為淨應付所得稅金。

案例：

淨所得額(收入-費用)			1,000,000
不可扣除項項目			
罰金、罰款			20,000
不可抵扣之禮品費			5,000
總計			25,000
可抵扣項目			
廣告費用			70,000
員工薪資			70,000
折舊/攤銷			120,000
總計			510,000
應納稅所得額			490,000
所得稅率			
聯邦所得稅	15%		73,500
BC省所得稅	11%		53,900
應付稅金			127,400

二、集團申報：

集團旗下有眾多公司，因每個公司均為獨立個體應獨立申報，不得以合併方式申報所得稅。

三、納稅年度：公司納稅年度不得超過53週。

肆、申報規範：

加拿大稅務法規定所得稅最終繳納期限不得晚於納稅年度結束後的第2個月。

公司所得稅申報表(T3所得稅報表)應於納稅年度結束後6個月內提交。當然也有例外情形，例如：

信託公司：必須在納稅年度結束後90日內提交，但沒有應納稅所得額且未進行受益人分配除外。

伍、罰款：

逾期未進行納稅申報將會受到處罰。納稅申報時，應納稅所得額應包括漏繳稅款，過失虛假陳述中也應體現漏繳數額。未按要求履行代扣代繳義務也將受到稅務機關的處罰。

第五節 公司帳務

壹、加拿大公司會計制度概述：

　　通常需要透過會計制度來了解公司營運狀況，且依法必須向政府繳納公司所得稅。

加拿大會計制度可分為應計法及現金法：

■**現金法(Cash Method)**：漁民，農場主或自僱者所採用，以實際收到的收入和實際支出的費用為主。

■**應計法(Accrual Method)**：一般營業人所採用，無論是否實際收到收入，只需考量已賺取之收入、存貨、費用及應收應付帳款等。

貳、公司銀行帳戶及開立支票：

　　公司於支付款項時，盡可能使用公司帳戶內金錢或開立支票，記帳時應記載支票號碼和日期。

加拿大公司戶開立支票應記載下列內容：

✓ 收款人姓名或公司名稱

✓ 付款目的

✓ 付款日期

✓ 支付金額

✓ GST金額

參、零用金：

支付公司小額支出或臨時性雜費支出時，可設置公司零用金機制做付款，零用金的支出也必須保留原始憑證。

肆、汽車利益(Standby Charge)：

一、公司買車：

公司以公司名義購買汽車給員工作為公務車使用，員工享有使用利益，此利益須計入收入，並繳納稅金，汽車無論折舊為何，汽車利益以汽車原價計算之。

汽車利益包含備用費(Standby Charges)及運作費(Operating Cast)，如：汽油、維修、牌照費及保險費等。

　　為了簡化運作費計算，如50%以上作為公務車使用，運作費為備用費的二分之一。

■備用費的計算方式：

　　每年備用費=汽車原價(含稅) x 2% x 12

■運作成本計算方式：

　　運作費=每年備用費 x 0.5

■例：

　　汽車原價30,000加幣(含稅)

　　備用費(Standby Charges)=30,000 x 2% x 12=7,200加幣

　　運作成本(Operating Cost)=7,200^0.5=3,600加幣

　　汽車利益=7,200 + 3,600 = 10,800加幣

　　自2019年後，運作成本可依每公里0.28加幣計算(50%以上作為公務車使用)。

■例：

　　汽車原價30,000加幣(含稅)

　　汽車全年總公里數為35,000km

　　個人使用比例為40%(即使用公里數14,000km)

　　備用費(Standby Charges)=30,000 x 2% x 12=7,200加幣

　　運作成本(Operating Cost)=14,000 km x 0.28 = 3,920加幣

　　汽車利益=7,200 + 3,920 = 11,120加幣

二、公司租車：

公司以公司名義承租汽車給員工作為公務車使用，汽車利益改以租金計算之。

■備用費的計算方式：

每年備用費=汽車租金 x 2/3

■運作成本計算方式：

運作費=每年備用費 x 1.5

■例：

汽車租賃費一年12,000加幣

備用費(Standby Charges)=12,000 x 2/3=8,000加幣

運作成本(Operating Cost)=8,000*1.5=12,000加幣

汽車利益=8,000 + 12,000 = 20,000加幣

三、如何降低汽車利益：

自2003年起，汽車50%以上之公里數作為公務車使用，且私人使用每年低於20,000公里，汽車利益得減低：

■計算方式：

(原汽車利益 x 私人使用公里數)/20,000

■例：

每年私人使用公里數為5,000 km，原汽車利益為10,000加幣

汽車利益可減為：

10,000 x 5,000 / 20,000 =2,500加幣

需注意的是，從住家到公司之間里程數僅能作為私人使用。

四、員工自購汽車：

員工自購汽車作為公務車使用，公司可依里程數補貼員工：

■里程數5,000 km以下：每公里補貼0.61加幣

■里程數5,000 km以上：每公里補貼0.55加幣。

■例：

員工自購汽車作為公務車用里程數為10,000 km，公司可補貼：

(5,000 x 61) + (5,000 x 55)=5,800加幣

員工自購車補貼不得做為員工收入，僅可作為公司費用抵扣所得稅，因此公司如有公務車使用之需求，可以由員工自購汽車，補助之費用非但不用計入員工個人所得，公司亦可以做為費用抵扣公司所得稅。

五、GST退稅：

員工自購汽車作為公務車用，且自行負擔運作成本，GST稅額支出的部分員工得於申報個人所得稅時，得向加拿大稅務局申請退還作為公務車用的GST，四年內均可申請退稅，且於收到GST

退稅稅金後，應計入下年度個人所得稅申報。

■例：

員工自購車60%作為公務車用

油資：100 x 60% =60加幣

GST退稅：60 x 5% =3加幣

維修費：2,000 x 60% =1,200加幣

GST退稅：1,200 x 5% =60加幣

貶值：3,000 x 60% =1,800加幣

GST退稅：1,800 x 5% =90加幣

第六節　非加拿大之境外公司

壹、加拿大境外公司稅收概述：

一般來說加拿大公司於加拿大境內從事商業活動之收入，應計入所得並向加拿大稅務局申報所得稅；境外公司在加拿大從事商業活動是否也需要申報所得稅呢？

一、境外公司認定：

1.加拿大公司：

公司於加拿大設立

管理核心及公司掌控權位於加拿大

2.非加拿大之境外公司：以上條件以外之公司。

二、應申報所得稅之境外公司：

非加拿大之境外公司被認定為在加拿大從事商業活動會被要求向加拿大稅務局申報聯邦所得稅和省的所得稅：

1. 在加拿大從事生產、栽種、採礦、製造、裝配、改良、包裝、保存或建設等。
2. 在加拿大販售，或透過分公司、代理商從事營運。

貳、加拿大境外公司申報所得稅：

一、申報方法及稅率：

境外公司通常採用「預提所得稅」方法來申報所得稅，稅率同加拿大稅法的一般稅率。此外，境外公司之分公司也應繳納「預提所得稅」，稅率為25%。

有些國家會透過與加拿大簽訂境外公司稅收協議來訂定適用的

稅率，如加拿大與美國就有簽訂稅收協議，美國公司在加拿大設立分公司適用的所得稅率為5%。

境外公司處分加拿大應稅財產之獲利也應繳納加拿大納稅，應稅財產如下：

1. 位於加拿大之不動產。

2. 在加拿大從事商業活動使用的資產。

3. 持有加拿大的私人公司股權，且5年內該股權50%以上的價值來自於加拿大的不動產。

4. 持有加拿大上市公司25%以上股權，且5年內，且5年內該股權50%以上的價值來自於加拿大的不動產。

5. 合夥公司持有之資產和現金市價50%以上由特定類型的加拿大資產組成，且5年內該資產50%以上的價值來自於加拿大的不動產。

6. 於加拿大之信託財產(共同信託基金除外，除非境外公司持有25%以上之共同信託基金)，且5年內該信託財產50%以上的價值來自於加拿大的不動產。

7. 持有非加拿大公司股權(在加拿大以外之證券交易所上市的股票除外)，該股權50%以上的價值來自於加拿大的不動產或資產。

二、預提所得稅：

境外公司需繳納預提所得稅之項目如下，除國家間有簽署稅收協議外，預提所得稅稅率為25%：

1.紅利

2.利息

3.特許使用費

例外免徵預提所得稅之項目：

文學、戲劇、音樂、藝術創作等著作權獲得的特許使用費，但電影版權、影像版權或其他與電影電視相關版權不適用之。

4.技術服務費

5.分支機構匯款稅

6.社會保險：

包含雇用員工之就業保險(EI)和加拿大退休金(CPP)等須依法繳納費用。

7.其他：

租賃收入和管理費：稅率25%。

■因使用位於加拿大資產而支付的租金

■境外公司主要營運活動包含製造、加工位於加拿大。

專利、商標、機密程式設計或專有技術使用權費用。

第七節 加拿大稅務表單

　　加拿大報稅用表可以從郵局取得，可領取一份報稅表及一份報稅指南，所有報稅表格都一式二份，一份提交加拿大稅務局，一份自己留底。

■T1報稅表：個人或自雇人士申報個人所得稅使用。

■T2報稅表：申報公司稅務使用。

■T3報稅表：國內外股票、債券、利息等收益申報使用。

■T4報稅表：員工薪資所得收入申報使用。

■T4A報稅表：退休金、年金收入申報使用。

■T4A(OAS) 報稅表：老金收入(Old Age Security)申報使用。

■T4A(P)報稅表：加拿大退休金計劃(CPP)申報使用。

■T4E報稅表：就業保險(EI)收入申報使用。

■T4RIF報稅表：退休收入基金(RRF)申報使用。

■T4RSP報稅表：退休計劃(RRSP)收入申報使用。

■T5報稅表：投資收入申報使用。

第八節　健康福利信託 (HWT)

壹、概述：

　　此為加拿大稅務局認可的醫療健康計劃之一，HWT是一種特定的信託，用於為公司員工支付醫療保健費用，僱主所支付的費用可用來減稅，而此費用支出不須計入員工之收入。

　　此信託當事人關係為雇主、管理人和受託人，一般來說HWT的資金無法退還給雇主或用於健康福利以外目的，雇主支付之款項不得超過健康福利所需的金額，一旦支付保單款項後即不能做更改。

　　健康福利信託適合一般小型公司，優點如下：

1.員工家屬享有不包括於政府醫療保險計劃內之醫療服務，例如牙醫及高單價配方藥物。

2.可享有私人醫院住院治療。

3.相較一般團體醫療保險 (Group Insurance)來得便宜。

4.可自由選擇不同的賠償額度，彈性較大。例如雇主可選擇享有無上限的賠償額度，而員工享有限額度之賠償金，限額也是由雇主自行決定。

貳、成立條件及限制：

加拿大稅局規定要成立一個健康福利信託，必須由第三方獨立信託機構負責管理。一般的信託機構登記費用為200加幣，管理費用為醫療費10%。公司成立健康福利信託時，可提供予不同員工及其家屬醫療福利的詳細說明。

此所稱之家屬包含員工之配偶、受撫養子女或孫子女，或是員工之其他親屬須為加拿大居民，例如父母、祖父母、兄弟姐妹、叔叔、阿姨、侄女或侄子等。

雇主應在「計劃年度」內向信託機構支付供款金額，該款項金額應依員工提供之勞動服務為合理之金額，但不得超過提供福利所需的金額。

供款金額為年度申報，在十二個月的保單年度內不得修改供款金額，除非員工生活有重大變化，受託人可以強制雇主在保單年度內支付供款。

保單年度開始後會設定新的供款額度，如果支出金額少於供款金額，未使用的金額可以轉到下一年度。

參、承保範圍：

HWT承保範圍包括的項目如下：

■處方藥、藥物和維生素：

如由員工及其配偶或其受撫養人購買，並由醫生開立處方及藥劑師記錄，則符合承保範圍；但如果維生素是有醫生處方，但並非從處方紀錄之藥劑師處所購買，則該費用不符合承保範圍。

■眼鏡(有醫生處方)、眼睛雷射

■牙科：

支付給牙醫、牙科保健員、牙科外科醫生或牙科技工的費用且用於診斷、治療或康復服務的範圍內者，均符合承保範圍。

■專業醫療服務：

脊椎醫生、聽力治療、皮膚科醫師、營養師、骨科醫師、物理治療師、足病醫生、精神科醫生、心理分析師、心理醫師、內科醫生和外科醫生、放射科醫生、按摩治療師、助產士、神經科醫生、職業治療師、言語治療師、護士、呼吸治療師、自然療法

■整容手術：

「純美容」不符合承保範圍。

■交通費用：

除往返醫院的救護車費用外(距離40公里以上)，還包括將患者和護理人員送至診所、醫院服務，如果距離超過80公里以上，膳食和住宿費用亦符合承保範圍。

■保險費：

支付給非政府醫療計劃的保費符合承保範圍。

第五章

置產
相關稅務

　　新移民入境加拿大時，面對食衣住行文化的差異，大多會感到不適應，其中所面臨到的第一個難題便是居住地點，選定好要落腳的城市之後，初期大多會選擇租房的方式，不僅可以藉此熟悉環境，也可以避免倉促決定買下不如意的房子，但是長遠來看，新移民既然要在加拿大定居下來，勢必需要置產來擁有自己的房子，本章節介紹加拿大自住置產時會遇到的種種問題。

第一節 置產自住

　　溫哥華和多倫多是加拿大移民人口最多的城市，尤其是溫哥華，華人移民占溫哥華整個城市人口比例約30%。受自然環境和教育資源等有利條件所吸引，近年來到加拿大置產的新移民買家也越來越多，而在加拿大置產與在台灣有什麼差別呢？

壹、台灣V.S.加拿大購屋稅率比較：

一、台灣：

　　在台灣購買房屋時，不動產買賣不只房地本身交易金額，買方需支付的金額除了頭期款以外，還須預留台幣數十萬元的稅金，包括契稅、印花稅、地政登記規費、貸款設定登記費等等。

■**印花稅：**

向地政機關申請物權登記之契據。

➡ （房屋評定現值＋土地公告現值）＊0.1%

■**契稅：**當不動產發生移轉時，買方需要繳納的費用。

→房屋評定現值＊6%

■**登記規費：**

地政事務所辦理土地及建物移轉登記規費。

➡ （房屋評定現值＋土地公告現值）＊0.1%

■**貸款設定登記費：**

貸款辦理設定時登記費。

➡貸款金額＊1.2＊0.1%

舉例：

以一間交易價格台幣2000萬元不動產為例，土地公告現值台幣300萬元，土地申報地價台幣60萬元，房屋評定現值台幣200萬元，貸款金額台幣1600萬元。	
契稅	200萬 X 6% = 12萬
印花稅	(300萬＋200萬) X 0.1% = 5,000
地政登記規費	(60萬＋200萬) X 0.1% = 2,600
貸款設定登記費	1600萬 X 0.12% = 19,200
合計	台幣146,800元

二、加拿大：

在加拿大購買房屋時，不動產買賣不只房地本身交易金額，買方需支付的金額除了頭期款以外，還須預留2~10萬元的稅金，包括物業交易稅、地稅、新房購置消費稅等等。

■物業交易稅（Property Transfer Tax）：

無論新房還是二手屋，過戶的時候都要先繳納此稅。

➡房價*稅率

房價	稅率
20萬以下	1%
超過20萬部分~200萬	2%
超過200萬部分~300萬	3%
超過300萬部分	5%

■地稅（Property Tax）：

加拿大是土地私有制的國家，地稅稅率依每個城市訂出下一年度財政預算後，再依房產基數去分攤費用，類似台灣的房屋稅。

➡依每個城市算法不同，以400萬的房屋為例，地稅約為1萬元左右。

■BC省學校稅（Additional School Tax）：

地稅的一種，只有在BC省價值超過300萬的房屋需繳納此稅。

➡房價*稅率

房價	稅率
300萬以下	免徵
超過300萬部分~400萬	0.2%
超過400萬部分	0.4%

■新房購置商品及服務稅（Goods and services Tax）：

在加拿大買東西都要交商品及服務稅的，買房當然也不例外，但是只有新房在第一次交易時需繳納消費稅，第二次交易起即不須繳納。

→房價*5%

課稅退還

為了減輕購置新屋的負擔，加拿大政府設立了GST退還機制，當購買$ 350,000以下新屋時，可以退回已繳GST的36%，最多為$ 6,300；購買$ 350,000~$ 450,000的新屋時，最多可退回稅金會遞減；購買超過$ 450,000新屋則不退回已繳GST。

■銷售稅(HST)：

在加拿大買東西都要交HST的，買房當然也不例外，但是只有新房在第一次交易時需繳納消費稅，二手屋即不須繳納。若是與買賣房屋相關的服務費用，仍需繳納HST，例如律師費、仲介佣金、搬家費、驗屋費、估價費等等。

➡房價*13%

■多倫多土地轉讓稅：

如果在多倫多地區購買房屋，需額外繳納多倫多土地轉讓稅以及安省土地轉讓稅。

➡房價*稅率

安省土地轉讓稅

房價	稅率
5.5萬以下	0.5%
超過5.5萬部分~25萬	1%
超過25萬部分~40萬	1.5%
超過40萬部分	2%

多倫多土地轉讓稅

房價	稅率
5.5萬以下	0.5%
超過5.5萬部分~40萬	1%
超過40萬部分~4000萬	1.5%
	2%(小面積獨棟)
超過4000萬部分	1%
	2%(小面積獨棟)

舉例：

以一間交易價格100萬元的二手不動產為例。	
物業交易稅	20萬X 1%+80萬X 2% = 18,000
地稅	3,000
合計	21,000元

貳、房屋稅可抵免費用：

加拿大身為高福利高稅收大國，若是因房屋產生了相關收入當然也需要申報所得稅，但是其中已支出的費用部分是可以抵稅的，就算房屋沒有產生收入，當年度有房屋相關支出，也是可以列報抵免喔！

一、租金收入：

將房屋出租所產生的租金收入，有以下可抵免費用：

■利息費用

➡包括購屋貸款利息、裝修貸款利息、購置家具刷卡利息等等。

■房屋稅

➡依房屋出租比例抵免，自住部份不能抵免。

■日常維修費用

➡正常且必要的維修保養，包括油漆粉刷、水電維修、更換破損物品等等。

■交通費用

➡因出租房屋而產生之合理交通費用。

■水電費用

居家辦公費用

➡居家辦公處理房屋出租相關事宜。

■薪資費用

➡聘請員工處理出租房屋事宜所產生之薪資費用。

■意外損失

➡因地震、火災、失竊等意外損失，可抵免金額視損失程度及保險範圍而定。

■保險費用

■管理費用

■廣告費用

二、買房抵免所得稅：

當年度有購置房屋時，滿足以下條件可以享有 $ 750的抵免額度：

✓ 申請人及配偶近4年名下無房產

✓ 如家裡有殘疾人士，購屋是為了使其生活更方便，則不受4
年無房產限制。

三、安省老年人房屋稅抵免

(Ontario Senior HomeownersProperty Tax Grant)：

凡年滿64歲以上老人繳納自有房屋稅，滿足中低收入戶的條
件，即可申請最多$ 500抵免額度，一對夫婦只能申請一筆。

淨收入	可抵免額度
$ 35,000	$ 500
$ 35,000~ $ 49,985	$1~500
超過$ 49,985	$ 0

四、安省能源與財產稅抵免

(Ontario Energy and Property Tax Credit)：

安省居民擁有或出租一間房屋，可獲得最多 $ 900的能源與財產稅抵免，老年人則可獲得最多 $ 1,025的能源與財產稅抵免。

五、裝修費用抵免：

為鼓勵屋主汰舊換新，加強老屋翻修，創造更安全、節能的居住環境，裝修費用也可依一定比例抵免應納稅金。

六、搬家費用抵免：

若是因為換了新工作、新學校而搬遷了40公里以外的新家，則搬家費用也可以抵稅，包括搬家期間合理支出的餐費、交通費、住宿費、處理舊家所產生的費用等等。

參、首次置產福利

首次購房者激勵計劃幫助加拿大各地的人們購買他們的第一套房子。該計劃提供房屋購買價格的 5%~10% 用於支付頭期款。並提供房價的5%~10%額度的抵押貸款，這降低了需要借款的金額，減少每月還款壓力，使購房更實惠。

✓ 申請資格

✓ 從未買過房子

✓ 過去4年未居住過配偶擁有的房子

✓ 最近經歷婚姻破裂

✓ 年收入總額不超過 $ 120,000（如果您購買的房屋位於多倫多、溫哥華或維多利亞，則為 $ 150,000）

✓ 借款總額不超過您的收入的 4 倍（如果您購買的房屋位於多倫多、溫哥華或維多利亞，則為 4.5 倍）

✓ 自有資金滿足最低首付要求

第二節 投資房產

　　在多數華人的觀念中，都有將財富傳承給下一代的想法，包括自己的現金、不動產、投資等等，要傳承必須先創造財富，擁有一定金額的財富才能維持自己老年生活品質及傳承給子女衣食無慮的生活，說到創造財富免不了就是投資，其中置產是很多人選擇的投資方式，不僅買房出租立即就能有收入，房價更是高機率會隨著時間增長，若是未來養老時更可以保有一個屬於自己的房子退休。

壹、台灣V.S.加拿大投資成本比較：

一、台灣：

在台灣持有房屋時，每年需繳納房屋稅及地價稅。

■房屋稅

➡房屋評定現值*稅率

房屋使用情況	房屋稅稅率
自住	1.2%
其他供住家用者	1.5~3.6%
營業用	3%~5%
非營業用	1.5%~2.5%

■地價稅

➡土地公告現值*稅率

土地使用情況	地價稅稅率
自住	0.2%
非自住	1%

舉例：

以一間交易價格台幣3000萬元自住不動產為例，土地申報地價台幣150萬元，房屋評定現值台幣50萬元。	
房屋稅	50萬X 1.2% = 6,000
地價稅	150萬X 0.2% = 3,000
合計	台幣9,000元

二、加拿大：

在加拿大持有房屋時，依各個省份規定不同每年須繳納不同稅率的空屋稅。

■溫哥華空屋稅（Vancouver Empty Home Tax）：

只要房屋在溫哥華不是自住用途，且1年中出租未滿6個月，即需繳納空屋稅。

→房價*3%(2021年稅率)

■BC省投機空置稅（B. C. Speculation and Vacancy Tax）：

只要房屋在BC省不是自住用途，且1年中出租未滿6個月，即需繳納空屋稅，就算是BC省非居民、加拿大非居民、居住在海外的BC省居民都須繳納。

➡房價*稅率

身分	稅率
加拿大居民	0.5%
加拿大非居民	2%

■**溫哥華海外買家稅（Additional Property Transfer Tax）：**

　海外買家購屋需額外繳納此筆稅金。

➡房價*20%

■**安省非居民投機稅(Non-Resident Speculation Tax)：**

針對買房卻不自住也不出租的加拿大非居民屋主課徵房屋空置稅。若是在購屋後4年成為永久居民、就學2年以上的合法留學生或工作1年以上的工作者，則將會退還此稅金。

➡房價*20%

■**資產增值稅：**

針對非居民或持有空屋課徵資產增值稅，繼承遺產時也常發生鉅額資產增值稅問題。

➡增值部分*23%

■地稅（Property Tax）：

加拿大是土地私有制的國家，地稅稅率依每個城市訂出下一年度
財政預算後，再依房產基數去分攤費用，類似台灣的房屋稅。

➡依每個城市算法不同，以400萬的房屋為例，地稅約為1萬元
左右。

舉例：

以一間交易價格300萬元位於安省的二手不動產為例，屋主非加拿大居民，房屋今年增值20萬，持有房屋成本？	
安省非居民投機稅(購買時)	300萬X 15% = 450,000
資產增值稅(出售時)	20萬 X 23% = 46,000
地稅	8,000
合計	$ 504,000

貳、海外買家購屋：

在加拿大買房通常有四大目的：自住、度假用、出租用及
投資用。加拿大居民可擁有一間出售時免稅的自住房屋，其餘
名下的其他房產在稅務上都視為投資用途。而當這些投資用途
房屋出售時，若是已經長期持有，其出售獲利一般可以資本利得
（Capital Gain）報稅，只有50%計入所得。

■海外買家在加拿大買房與當地居民區別

1.以下以位於溫哥華價格300萬的二手房屋為例,今年漲價20
萬,非自住或出租用途:

購屋差異

	海外買家	加拿大居民
物業交易稅	20萬*1%+180萬*2%+100萬*3% = 68,000	
溫哥華海外買家稅	300萬*20% = 60萬	0
合計	$ 668,000	$ 68,000

持有差異

	海外買家	加拿大居民
地稅	8,000	
溫哥華空屋稅	300萬*1.75% = 52,500	
BC省投機空置稅	300萬*2% = 60,000	300萬*0.5% = 15,000
合計	$ 120,500	$ 75,500

出售差異

	海外買家	加拿大居民
資產增值稅	20萬*23% = 46,000	
合計	$ 46,000	

2.以下以位於多倫多價格300萬的二手房屋為例，今年漲價20
萬，非自住或出租用途：

購屋差異

	海外買家	加拿大居民
物業交易稅	20萬*1%+180萬*2%+100萬*3% = 68,000	
多倫多土地轉讓稅	5.5萬*0.5%+34.5萬*1%+260萬*1.5% = 42,725	
安省土地轉讓稅	5.5萬*0.5%+19.5萬*1%+15萬*1.5%+260萬*2% = 56,475	
合計	$ 167,200	

持有差異

	海外買家	加拿大居民
地稅	8,000	
安省非居民投機稅	300萬*20% = 600,000	0
合計	$ 608,000	$ 8,000

出售差異

	海外買家	加拿大居民
資產增值稅	20萬*23% = 46,000	
合計	$ 46,000	

第三節 其他投資商品

除了置產投資以外，還有許多投資產品可以做資產規劃，以下僅介紹穩健類金融商品如股票、債券、共同基金(Mutual Funds)、股票型基金 Exchange Traded Funds (ETF)、保本基金 Segregated Funds (SF)等等，投機性商品如期權交易等則不贅述。

壹、共同基金(Mutual Funds)：

共同基金是一種將眾多投資人的資金匯集起來再按照基金目標進行投資的投資方式，會有專業的投資經理代表投資者進行各項投資決定，例如：股票、債券、貨幣交易等等，依照投資者購買基金比例來分配未來獲利比例，獲利包括利息、股息、資產增值都會按比例分攤給投資者。每日基金的單位價格按每日基金內所有投資項目市場價格而定，將總市值扣除部分費用後再除以單位總數，就是當日的基金單位價格。投資皆有風險性，應謹慎評估挑選近3~5年表現良好的基金，能降低投資失敗的風險。

▶優點

■有專業經理投資管理

➡可以省下研究投資項目的心力以及隨時追蹤投資市場的時間。

■分散風險

➡一次投資多種投資項目，使雞蛋不放在同一個籃子中，來達到分散風險的目的。

■資金靈活運用

➡比起定存或是置產，購買基金可以隨時買賣，臨時有急用時不會將資金綁死。

▶**種類**

■**貨幣型基金**

➡低風險低報酬的投資工具,適合存放短期資金,例如:外幣、國家債券。

■**配息基金**

➡定期發配利息的投資工具,報酬比貨幣型基金略高,但是也較容易隨著利率變動,例如:有固定配息的大企業債券、房貸抵押證券。

■**高報酬基金**

➡高報酬高風險的投資工具,目的在高報酬的投資方式,主要投資於股票。

■**分散風險基金**

➡投資各種高低風險的投資工具,適合剛開始投資想要分散投資風險的投資人。

貳、股票型基金
Exchange Traded Funds (ETF):

ETF其實也是基金的一個種類,所謂的基金就是幫你分散投資一籃子標的,標的可以是股票,也可以是債券或其他商品。雖然都是叫基金，但ETF這樣的基金商品，組成與買賣方式都和傳統的基金不太一樣。簡單來說就是把ETF當股票買賣，指數漲，ETF就會跟著漲，指數跌，ETF的價格也會跟著下跌。例如：台股知名的0050ETF就是追蹤臺灣50指數，這檔指數的成分股是台灣市值前50大上市公司的股票，買進這檔ETF，就等於一次買進這50間公司一部分的股票。你可以想像ETF是個水果籃，這個籃子裡有50種不同的水果，只買一種水果味道可能有好有壞，而買這個水果籃，你每一種水果都能吃到一點。

▶優點

■分散風險

➡一次購買眾多股票，不會因為某家績效不好而受到巨大損失。

■手續費低

➡因為不須專業管理，所以管理費用較一般基金便宜，也不用費心尋找績效好的管理團隊。

■買賣手續簡便

➡跟買賣股票一樣簡單方便，不論資金多寡的投資人都很適合。

參、保本基金 Segregated Funds (SF)：

　　SF是加拿大金融市場上一種獨特的投資產品，其服務對象為加拿大居民。非加拿大居民不能夠投資保本基金。保本基金與共同基金(Mutual Fund)相似，都是將投資者的資金籌集在一起，投資在證券組合上，故也常被認為是共同基金的一種;而跟共同基金不同的地方在於SF是專屬於保險公司才能發行的基金，因此此種基金是有保險的成分在裡面，若是投資者在基金到期前不幸去世，則保險公司會歸還已繳納的本金給基金受益人，不須經任何遺產手續；若是基金期滿，保險公司會歸還75%~100%的本金，因為保險公司須承擔一定的風險，因此收取的手續費也會較高。

▶優點

■還本

　　➡基金期滿保證還本75%~100%。

■轉嫁風險

　　➡若是投資者不幸過世，資金不會有大幅度損失。

■不受債務影響

　　➡若是投資者不幸過世，資金直接轉給受益人，不受投資者生前債務影響。

第六章

退休
稅務規劃

　　加拿大的退休保障體係是最完善的，聯邦政府把領取養老金的年齡和數額掛鈎，讓居民根據自己的情況，選擇加拿大移民提前60歲或者推遲到70歲再開始領取。這筆錢大部分取決於你在工作的時候的收入、養老金和居住時間。

 # 第一節 在加養老

壹、退休後的收入來源：

　　退休後沒有工作收入該如何維持老年生活品質呢?加拿大公民退休後主要收入來源有養老金、配偶津貼、遺孀津貼、加拿大退休金及註冊退休儲蓄計畫等等，以下介紹七個常見的退休收入來源：

一、老人年金(Old Age Security ,OAS)：

　　OAS是加拿大政府按月支付給65歲以上，屬於加拿大公民或合法居民的老年人福利。要獲得最高的OAS金額，則需在加拿大居住了40年以上（18歲以後）。

▶申請資格

✓ 18歲以後在加拿大境內住滿10年

✓ 年滿65歲(2023年4月開始須年滿67歲)

✓ 加拿大公民或永久居民

✓ 居住在加拿大

▶申請金額

金額的大小與住在加拿大的時間有關,18歲以後在加拿大境內住滿40年,65~74歲每月可以領取最高金額 $ 685.5,75歲以上每月可以領取最高金額 $ 754.05,若是僅住滿10年,則依比例計算領取1/4金額;住滿 20 年以上,則可以在加拿大以外的地區領取老人年金。

若是選擇延遲領取養老金,最長可以延遲5年至70歲領取,每月可增加0.6%,5年最多可以增加36%。

年收入在 $ 80,000以下可以領取最多金額;年收入在 $ 80,000~ $ 130,000之間則隨著收入增加而遞減;年收入超過 $ 130,000則無法領取養老金。

二、加拿大退休金計劃 (Canada Pension Plan,CPP):

加拿大退休金計劃為加拿大的確定給付制退休金制度,幾乎所有加拿大民眾都包含在此制度中，提撥部分由雇主跟員工分別提撥50%的費率，給付項目包括各式退休金給付、傷殘津貼、遺屬津貼，類似於我國勞保。

▶領取時間

標準領取養老金的年齡為65歲，最早可以60歲開始領取，則每月減少0.6%金額，最多減少36%養老金；最晚可以70歲領取，則每月增加0.7%金額，最多增加42%養老金。

▶領取金額

可領取金額取決於開始領取的年齡、提撥了多長時間以及提撥期間平均收入而定，最高每月可領取$1253.59。亦可將退休金分配最多一半給配偶，達到分散收入的目的。

三、保證收入補助金 (GIS)：

GIS是OAS計劃的一部分，只有領取養老金(OAS)的人才可有資格申請GIS，是提供給低收入老年人的一種收入補助。

▶申請資格

✓ 年滿65歲

✓ 居住在加拿大

✓ 已經在領取老人年金OAS

✓ 收入低於GIS標準

婚姻狀況	家庭年收入	每月最多可領取金額
單身	低於 $ 20,784	$ 1,023.88
配偶有領取OAS	低於 $ 27,456	$ 616.31
配偶有領取 60-64津貼	低於 $ 38,448	$ 616.31
配偶沒有領取OAS	低於 $ 49,824	$ 1,023.88

四、保證收入補助金 (GIS) -配偶津貼：

這是OAS計劃下的福利，支付給年齡在60歲至64歲之間的低收入老年人，一旦年滿65歲停止，即轉為領取老人年金OAS，屬於一種臨時性的福利。

▶申請資格

✓ 年齡60~64歲(2023年4月之後，年齡須介於62~64歲之間)

✓ 18歲以後在加拿大住滿10年

✓ 配偶是OAS和GIS的受益人

✓ 收入低於GIS標準

婚姻狀況	家庭年收入	每月最多可領取金額
配偶或伴侶領取OAS 和GIS全額補助金	低於 $ 38,448	$ 1,301.81

五、保證收入補助金 (GIS) -遺孀：

這是OAS計劃下的福利，支付給年齡在60歲至64歲之間的遺孀，一旦年滿65歲停止，即轉為領取老人年金OAS，屬於一種臨時性的福利。

▶申請資格

✓ 年齡60~64歲(2023年4月之後，年齡須介於62~64歲之間)

✓ 配偶是OAS和GIS的受益人

✓ 曾經居住加拿大超過10年

✓ 配偶已過世且未再婚

✓ 收入低於GIS標準

婚姻狀況	年收入	每月最多可領取金額
遺孀	低於 $ 27,984	$ 1,551.85

六、註冊退休儲蓄計劃 (RRSP)：

註冊退休儲蓄計劃 (RRSP) 是一種在加拿大政府註冊的儲蓄計

劃，鼓勵您做儲蓄以保障您的退休生活。此外，當您向RRSP存款時，您的資金可享受「稅收優惠」，這代表在您存款的那一年，存款可以免稅，但是每年存款額度是有限的。隨後，只要這筆資金保留在RRSP內，RRSP持有的投資在取款之前賺取的任何投資收入都可以免稅，延遲到取款時再列為收入。而由於退休後提領時的收入可能比在職時少很多，因此可以適用較低的稅率，就可以為您省較多稅款。至於帳戶內的可以隨個人決定如何使用，並無限制。可以持續存款至年滿71歲，若是配偶尚未年滿71歲，則可以存款至配偶的RRSP帳戶內，達到分散收入的目的。

▶**申請資格**

年滿18歲以上加拿大居民

▶**存款限額**

若是沒有其他公司註冊的退休計畫，則限額為去年勞工收入的18%或是以下限額(取低者)。

年度	限額
2022年	$ 29,210
2021年	$ 27,830
2020年	$ 27,230
2019年	$ 26,500
2018年	$ 26,230
2017年	$ 26,010

▶提領方式
■一次領取
➡一次領取帳戶中所有金額，但是提取金額全數須列報當年度收入報稅，因此一次領取可能需要支付最高所得稅稅率。

■年金領取
➡將帳戶中金額轉移到財務機構，依照個人需求分為10年期、20年期或是終身年金，期限越短，每次可提取金額越多，每年提取金額須列報收入報稅。

■註冊退休入息基金
Registered Retirement Income Fund (RRIF)
➡將帳戶中金額轉移到另一個註冊退休入息基金(RRIF)帳戶，這是一個不能存款的帳戶，一旦轉入後須依照政府規定每年領取金額。

七、反向房屋貸款(Reverse Mortgage)：
對於擁有房屋的退休人士來說，反向房屋貸款也可以算是一筆退休收入，透過將房屋抵押給金融機構，來獲得貸款支應退休費用，一般來說可以貸到房屋價值約10~40%左右，唯一規定是必須年滿62歲才能申請，年紀越大可以貸款金額越多，屋主不必每月還款，只須待未來房屋出售時再一併償還本金及利息即可。

貳、遺產規劃：

在加拿大不論是聯邦或是省政府都沒有課徵遺產稅，但是每個人離世時，稅務局視同該納稅人以離世前一天的市場價值，將其名下的所有資產都出售了，再轉給繼承人，但是遺產傳承給子女時可能會有高額資產增值稅，以及遺產檢驗相關費用，為避免一次性須支付大筆稅金，退休人士需要及早做好遺產規劃。

一、個人所得稅：

當納稅人過世時，名下所有資產都須認作是以當日市價出售，除了遺贈給配偶的部分可以認定使用原取得成本轉讓，其餘認定當日出售的資產都會依資產增值幅度課徵資產增值稅。

二、註冊退休儲蓄計劃 (RRSP)：

RRSP剩餘的儲蓄金額需全部列為故人的收入，若是由配偶或未成年子女承接則須列為承接人收入，除非配偶將金額轉進自己名下的RRSP，子孫轉為購買年金至18歲成年，則可以暫緩列入收入。

三、檢驗遺囑費（Probate fees）：

在加拿大依遺產的額度徵收檢驗遺囑費，以B.C.省為例，

遺產價值 $ 25,000以下免收此筆費用；遺產價值 $ 25,000~
$ 50,000部分為0.6%；超過 $ 50,000部分為1.4%。舉例
來說，遺產總價值 $ 80,000須收取$ 570的檢驗遺囑費。
(25,000*0.6%+30,000*1.4%)

遺產總額	B.C.省檢驗遺囑費
$ 25,000	免收
$ 25,000~ $ 50,000部分	0.6%
超過 $ 50,000部分	1.4%

參、返加退休：

曾經在加拿大定居或工作的居民，因各種因素返回原國家生
活，退休後想再回流加拿大居住，有哪些稅務問題是需要注意的
呢？回流加拿大的居民只要重新成為「稅務居民」（resident）
後，都必須申報相關的退休金與海外收入。

▶回流加拿大應納稅身分

　✓ 一年住滿183天

　✓ 擁有加拿大房屋

　✓ 在加拿大有配偶一起撫養未成年子女

　✓ 有駕照、醫療保險、銀行帳戶等等生活連結

▶**應申報收入**

　✓ 加拿大收入

　✓ 海外收入

　✓ 資產增值收入

肆、節稅方式：

一、分散收入：

　按照加拿大的稅收制度，收入越高適用的稅率越高，因此若是能把收入分攤給家中收入較低的成員，就能利用每個家庭成員的免稅額及低稅率，讓家庭收入得以課徵較低的所得稅率，減輕家庭稅賦負擔，這是透過分散收入達成節稅的目的。

▶**節稅方式**

1. 透過贈與將資產轉移給18歲以上子女，則資產所得收入會轉由子女報稅，需注意的是，資產轉移的過程可能會有資產增值稅的問題。

2. 每月收到的子女養育金存入子女個人帳戶，則所產生的利息收入不需由父母報稅。

3. 高收入的配偶支付家庭中大部分開銷，並替低收入配偶儲蓄RRSP 及TFSA。

4.儲蓄註冊教育儲蓄計畫

5.加拿大退休金CPP分配給配偶

二、增加扣除額：

透過增加每人可扣除額的額度，來進行節稅減輕所得稅金的負擔。

▶節稅方式

1.註冊退休儲蓄計劃 (RRSP)儲蓄至最高額度

2.托兒開支扣除額只能適用於低收入的配偶，而且可減稅的托兒開支是限於低收入配偶收入的2/3。

3.辦公費用扣除額適用於居家工作的申請人，可將部分家庭開銷視為辦公費用扣除。

Tips

節稅小撇步:

1.租稅協定-避免雙重課稅

2.善用免稅儲蓄戶口(TFSA)及退休儲蓄計劃(RRSP)

3.成本提升法-移民前墊高資產成本

4.收入分割-移民前妥善運用每個家庭成員的免稅額

5.分散收入-善用各收入來源扣除額

第二節 離加養老

取得加拿大公民身分後，因為語言、文化等差異或生涯規劃考量，有些人會選擇返回原居住國家退休養老，離開加拿大之後還是有身為加拿大公民應盡的義務以及能享有的福利，要如何才能避免海外收入被課稅呢？若是希望透過海外收入課稅並持續享有加拿大福利又應該注意什麼呢?

壹、不課稅不領福利-非稅務居民身分：

身為加拿大公民，就算長年居住在海外，只要跟加拿大有生活連結或是配偶子女在加拿大生活，就屬於加拿人稅務居民，全球收入仍然需要課徵所得稅，包括薪資收入、經商收入、投資收益、利息收入等等，若是不想要海外收入被加拿大稅務局課稅的話，除了須放棄福利以外，更須避免與加拿大產生聯繫。

▶**易被當作稅務居民課稅的重點**

  1.配偶及子女居住在加拿大境內

  2.名下有加拿大不動產，例如：房屋

  3.名下有加拿大動產，例如：汽車

4.離境後一年內再次入境加拿大

5.有加入加拿大各式社團會員

6.有還在使用中的加拿大銀行帳戶

7.持續領取福利金，例如：養老金

8.未通知CRA非稅務居民身分

9.未註銷加拿大電話號碼

10. 未結清註冊退休儲蓄帳戶

▶境內資產

當您轉變稅務身分為非居民時，CRA會將名下所有資產視為已變賣，並將出售利益的1/2作為應課稅收入。即使您沒有實際出售資產，您都需要在離境前支付所得稅金。

▶境內收入
■租金收入

若是非居民境內尚有房產出租中，則收到的租金收入需繳納25%作為扣除稅(Part XIII Tax)。

■退休金收入

若是非居民領取註冊儲蓄退休金，則需扣除25%稅金。

貳、課稅及領福利-稅務居民身分：

　　雖然離開加拿大在海外居住，但是還是可以享有加拿大的福利，可以透過與加拿大維繫生活連結，以及申報海外收入等方式，來維持加拿大稅務非居民身分並領取退休福利金OAS，但是若是全世界收入超該該年度的門檻時，需額外繳納15%的養老金收入回報。

▶收入門檻

年度	全球淨收入門檻
2021	$ 79,845
2020	$ 79,054
2019	$ 77,580
2018	$ 75,910
2017	$ 74,788
2016	$ 73,756
2015	$ 72,809

附　錄

常見名詞說明

■**Accrual Basis 權責發生制：**

會計制度的一種，又名應收應付制，以交易和事項是否實際發生為確認基礎，另一種是現金制。

■**Age Exemptions　65歲高齡扣除額：**

淨收入超過$38,900扣除額遞減，超過$90,000無扣除額。

■**Allowance 高齡配偶津貼：**

年齡介於60~64歲之低收入加拿大居民(2023年4月後改為62~64歲)，雖然尚未符合OAS及GIS請領年紀，但是若是配偶已在領取OAS及GIS補助，則可以請領此筆高齡配偶津貼，直至年滿65歲改為領取OAS及GIS補助。

■**Allowance for the Survivor 高齡遺孀津貼：**

年齡介於60~64歲之加拿大居民(2023年4月後改為62~64歲)，雖然尚未符合OAS及GIS請領年紀，但是配偶已過世，則遺孀可以領取此筆津貼，直至年滿65歲改為領取OAS及GIS補助。

■**Annuity 年金：**

RRSP的提領方式之一，將所有帳戶內資產轉至保險財務機構，可選擇終身年金，領取直至壽命終了；或是10年期、20年期等等，依提領人的需求去做規劃。

■**Business Income 營業所得：**

不論是獨資或合夥做生意的營運收入。

■**B.C. Speculation & Vacancy Tax B.C.省投機和空置稅：**

除了主要居所、出租用途、危樓等等原因外，B.C.省房屋閒置
會課徵0.5%~2%的空屋稅。

■**Calendar year 歷年制：**

每年1月1日起至12月31日止。

■**Capital Gains 資本所得：**

企業營運收入以外與企業資本相關收入，例如:通過出售房屋、
機器設備、股票、債券、商譽、商標和專利權等資本項目所獲
取的收入。

■**Child Care Expenses 育兒扣除額：**

撫養17歲以下兒童可減稅。

■**Canada Learning Bond 加拿大教育基金：**

針對2004年1月1日後出生並領有兒童補助的兒童，一次性發給
$500教育基金，每年另發給$100教育基金至15歲為止。

■**CPP(Canada Pension Plan) 加拿大退休金計劃：**

過去在加拿大工作期間有存款進此退休金帳戶，即可在滿65歲
時提領，60~65歲期間都可以申請提領，65歲以前提領需減少
提領金額，若是延遲至70歲提領，則可以領取多42%。

■**Deemed Resident 認定為居民：**

一年中逗留加拿大超過一百八十三日或是新移民。

■**Deemed Non-Resident 認定為非居民：**

一年中逗留加拿大少於一百八十三日或是與加拿大有稅務協議

之國家居民。

■**Deductible Interest 可減除利息：**

非購置私人資產所產生的利息可扣除，例如:貸款做生意。

■**Disability Amount 身心障礙扣除額：**

納稅人或受撫養親屬屬身心障礙人士可扣除額。

■**Dividend Received Deduction股利扣除額：**

　股利收入可享有稅務優惠，以B.C.省為例，如果僅有股利收

入，收入在$53,000以下可免徵所得稅。

■**Establish Residence 長住居住：**

經常習慣性居住於加拿大。

■**Employment Income 薪資所得：**

透過工作獲取的收入，包括獎金。

■**ETF(Exchange Traded Funds) 指數股票型基金：**

依股票指數市場中各成分股票做比例投資，不須專業經理人因

此管理費用較互惠基金便宜。

■**GIS(Guaranteed Income Supplement) 保證收入補助：**

加拿大政府針對領有OAS老年保障的居民，並且年收入低於

$16,800者可領取額外低收補助，以維持一定程度的生活水平。

■**GST(Goods & Services Tax) 貨品及服務稅：**

等同於營業稅，幾乎所有在加拿大買賣的商品及服務都需課徵
此稅。

■**GST Rebate 課稅退還：**

加拿大購買舊屋不須繳稅，購買新屋需繳GST，為減輕稅務
負擔，購買$350,000以下新屋可退還已繳GST的36%，超過
$350,000退還稅額會遞減，購買超過$450,000的新屋則不得退
還。

■**Home Buyers Plan 首次購屋計劃：**

規定購屋者或是配偶必須是屬於首次購屋自住，每個申請人可
以從他的RRSP中提取$35,000，夫妻共可提取$70,000，並於
15年內分期償還給RRSP，則此筆款項可以不作為收入提報。

■**Income Tax 所得稅：**

加拿大居民在全球各地的淨收入都須向加拿大政府納稅。

■**Investment Income 投資所得：**

透過財產獲取的收入，包括利息、股利、房產租金。

■**Individual Plan 自選的教育儲蓄計劃：**

將教育儲蓄金存入一般財務機構，可靈活更動受益人及額度，
對於投資策略也較有彈性。

■**In-trust Account 私人信託計劃：**

除了註冊教育儲蓄計劃可以分散收入以外，透過私人信託計劃也能達到分散收入給子女的目的，且不受額度、期限、提取限制。

■**Labor Income 勞工收入：**

包括薪資、租金等等，不包括利息收入。

■**Mutual Funds 共同基金：**

將個別投資者的資金聚集，再由專業經理人進行投資，基金所賺取的收益，依投資比例回饋給投資者。

■**Non-Deductible Interest 不可扣除利息：**

購置私人資產所產生利息不可扣除，例如:貸款買房自住。

■**Net Income 所得淨額：**

所得淨額 = 總收入來源 - 可扣除項目(RRSP退休儲蓄計畫、利息扣除額、育兒扣除額、其他扣除額)

■**Non-capital losses 非資本性虧損：**

與企業資本無關之虧損，可用來扣減課稅年度前三年或未來二十年收入。

■**Net-capital losses 資本性淨虧損：**

企業營運收入以外與企業資本相關虧損，可用來扣減課稅年度前三年或未來無限期收入。

■National Child Benefit 兒童福利金：

又稱牛奶金，低收家庭可以領取的養育津貼。

■Part-Year Resident 部分年度居民：

新移民入境後，依比例計算屬於加拿大居民期間。

■Personal Exemptions 個人扣除額：

可從所得淨額中扣減，包括基本扣除額、已婚扣除額、高齡扣
除額、殘疾扣除額、就業扣除額、學費扣除額等等。

■Pooled Plan 合資的教育儲蓄計劃：

將教育儲蓄金存入一已成立的教育基金，需填報受益人及每年
提取額度，較不靈活且投資較為保守。

■Probate fees 檢驗遺囑費：

加拿大無遺產稅，在過世後，政府僅會徵收一筆檢驗遺囑費。

■Property Transfer Tax 地產轉讓稅：

購置地產時需繳納地產轉讓稅，200,000以下課徵1%；
200,000~2,000,000課徵2%；2,000,000~3,000,000課徵3%；
3,000,000以上課徵5%。

■Reverse Mortgage 房屋抵押貸款：

退休後可以透過房屋抵押貸款獲取日常生活費用的一種方式，
年齡越高可獲得額度越大，屋主不須每月還款，待房屋出售時
再一次性償還本金及利息。

■**RRIF(Registered Retirement Income Fund)**
註冊退休收入基金：

　RRSP的提領方式之一，將所有帳戶內資產轉至另一個退休收入基金，RRIF與RRSP最大的不同在於不可存款，最早可於55歲時轉入RRIF帳戶，但是轉入後需開始每年提款。

■**RPP(Registered Pension Plan) 退休基金計劃：**

　由僱主提供的退休基金計劃，最高可獲得退休工資的70%，更可選擇分配一半收入給配偶，達到分散收入的好處。

■**Spousal Exemptions 已婚扣除額：**

　配偶收入在$13,808以下可扣除。

■**SF(Segregated Funds) 保本基金：**

　此種基金含有保險成分，本金分為基金部分及保險部分，因此期滿會依照合約規定至少退回本金75%。

■**Taxable Income 應稅所得：**

　淨收入扣除可減除項目後所得之金額。

■**Tax year 課稅年度：**

　應計算所得稅的期間。

■**Taxable Income 課稅所得：**

　課稅所得 = 所得淨額 - 個人免稅額(基本扣除額、已婚扣除額、高齡扣除額、殘疾扣除額、就業扣除額、學費扣除額)

■**Tuition Fees 學費扣除額：**

受撫養子女就學學費可扣除額。

■**Vancouver Empty Homes Tax 溫哥華房屋空置稅：**

除了主要居所、出租用途、危樓等等原因外，溫哥華房屋閒置

會課徵3%的空屋稅。

加拿大稅務輕鬆學 2023版

作　　者：廖建勳
編　　輯：張瑋恬、羅琪

出版者：理查移民股份有限公司
地　　址：台中市南屯區大進街490號10樓之3
電　　話：(04)2320-2153
傳　　真：(04)2320-8813
電子信箱：RicharRichLife@gmail.com
網　　址：https://richarrichlife-immi.com/

代理經銷：白象文化事業有限公司
地　　址：401台中市東區和平街228巷44號
電　　話：(04)2220-8589
傳　　真：(04)2220-8505

封面設計暨版面構成：波墨視覺設計有限公司
出版年月：中華民國112年1月
版　　次：初版
價　　格：新台幣300元整
ISBN　978-626-96978-0-9 (平裝)

國家圖書館出版品預行編目(CIP)資料

加拿大稅務輕鬆學 / 廖建勳著. --初版.
-- 臺中市：理查移民股份有限公司，民112.01
272面；14.8x21公分
ISBN　978-626-96978-0-9 (平裝)
1.CST：稅務　1.CST：移民　1.CST：加拿大
567.953　　　　　　　　　　　111021148